HOW DYNAMIC
IS *YOUR* SMALL GROUP?

HOW DYNAMIC
IS *YOUR* SMALL GROUP?

David P. Seemuth

VICTOR BOOKS®

A DIVISION OF SCRIPTURE PRESS PUBLICATIONS INC.
USA CANADA ENGLAND

Scripture quotations are from the *Holy Bible, New International Version,* © 1973, 1978, 1984, International Bible Society. Used by permission of Zondervan Bible Publishers. Other Scripture quotations are from *King James Version* (KJV) of the Bible.

Library of Congress Cataloging-in-Publication Data

Seemuth, David P.
  How dynamic is your small group? / by David P. Seemuth.
    p. cm.–(GroupBuilder resources)
    ISBN 0-89693-880-8
  1. Church group work. I. Title. II. Series.
BV652.2.S44   1991
253.7–dc20   91-15793
                                                       CIP

1 2 3 4 5 6 7 8 9 10 Printing / Year 95 94 93 92 91

CONTENTS

FOREWORD 7

PREFACE 9

CHAPTER ONE 11
Group Dynamics Make a Difference

CHAPTER TWO 17
The Small Group Dynamics Grid

CHAPTER THREE 28
An Atmosphere of Acceptance

CHAPTER FOUR 44
Groups with Purpose

CHAPTER FIVE 61
Communication for Edification

CHAPTER SIX 80
Developing Structures to Facilitate Groups

CHAPTER SEVEN 87
The Richness of People's Backgrounds

CHAPTER EIGHT 95
Cohesion: Glue to Bond People Together

CHAPTER NINE 103
Standards for Proceeding and Evaluating

CHAPTER TEN 110
The Small Group Life Cycle

CHAPTER ELEVEN 116
Putting It All Together

FOREWORD

Shortly after I became the pastor of Elmbrook Church, I was accosted in a supermarket by a lady who informed me that she had left my church. She went on to explain that we were not meeting her needs because the church was too big. In response to my question, "Did you ever indicate your needs to the church?" she admitted that she had not. However, she was adamant that the church had failed to meet her expectations and the reason was its size!

This encounter started me thinking — about the church in Jerusalem. Remember that they numbered approximately 5,000 but "were together." Their size and their fellowship were not mutually exclusive. For them there were no debates on big vs. small, evangelism vs. discipleship, spiritual nurture vs. social concern. They seemed to combine them all. But how? The records show that they met regularly for the apostles' teaching (presumably in large numbers) and from "house to house" (presumably in smaller groups). The former experiences allowed for corporate worship, evangelism, and teaching on a large scale, the latter for fellowship, caring, nurture, and personal attention of a more intimate dimension.

Armed with this insight, Elmbrook Church embarked on the development of a wide variety of small groups throughout the metropolitan area in which God has placed us. The results have been most gratifying, but that's another story!

Dr. David Seemuth has been involved in this work for many years, first as a layman, later as a student intern, and then as pastor of Small Group Ministries at Elmbrook Church. He has not only started groups, led them, trained leaders, gone troubleshooting, developed programs, written materials, read deeply, and taught seminars, but he has been deeply instrumental in the delicate task of taking groups and forming daughter churches from them. All this while completing a Ph.D. in New Testament!

In short, David knows what he's talking about because he has the mind of a scholar, the heart of a pastor, the experience of a practitioner, and he's working on the skin of a rhinoceros, which is sometimes helpful in this kind of work.

This book, his first, is eminently readable as it clearly enunciates principles liberally illustrated from real-life experience. It will prove to be immensely helpful to churches planning to start small groups, small groups whose "get up and go" has "got up and went" and also for small churches which are small groups themselves but who need help and encouragement in congregational life. By the way, healthy small groups tend to become large groups — we have a number of large small groups. They are a healthy contradiction in terms with their own set of problems. Nice ones, of course! Maybe David should write next about them.

D. Stuart Briscoe

PREFACE

"I can't imagine what people do who aren't in small groups at times of crises," declared the woman on the telephone. Her name was Kathy. One day earlier she had gone through an emergency hysterectomy moments after the birth of her third child. Her doctor credited the prayers of those in Kathy's small group for saving her life. Group members were praying at the hospital at her time of need. Soon they had teams of people for house cleaning, baby-sitting, and daily delivery of meals. In a word that small group was *dynamic*.

It is no wonder that I believe firmly in the importance and necessity of having small groups in local churches. But my goal is to have groups that are striving for excellence. And, thus, this book arose out of that desire to help groups attain their God-given potential. I hope it adds to the life of your small group.

Thanks are in order to the staff at Elmbrook Church, where I serve, and especially to Stuart Briscoe — a friend who has not ceased to encourage, challenge, and support me personally. Thanks also to Mike Frans, who was influential in my training and who, with his wife, Jan, developed many materials used in Elmbrook's small group training, some of which has been included here. I am grateful to my editor, Pam Campbell, who provided good suggestions, kindness, and patience. I appreciate the work Therese Crites did typing the manuscript. Finally, I thank my wife, Karen, for her encouragement and support. She's tops.

David P. Seemuth

ONE

GROUP DYNAMICS MAKE A DIFFERENCE

We put no stumbling block in anyone's path, so that our ministry will not be discredited (2 Corinthians 6:3).

Hello, my name is ... " said the name tag. Many of us have entered a room to be greeted with such a sight. *Such friendly people. I want to get to know them,* you automatically think. Or do you?

Look at the man standing in the corner. His arms are crossed in front of his chest. His face indicates he may have just attended the funeral of a close friend or perhaps lost his job. He is a bit fidgety, apparently waiting for the meeting to begin. The man is probably not a good candidate to risk introducing yourself to.

Next you glance at your hostess. She let you in the door, introduced herself to you, didn't wait to hear your name. That is understandable, though, because she is so busy preparing the coffee and answering the door. She did give you a name tag. How nice. Now, how does one find a pen in a place you have never been?

Ah ... here comes someone toward you to introduce himself. He has one of those name tags too! He walks right up to you and says, "Excuse me, can I squeeze by you? I need to get the songbooks out of the closet behind you." Had you only known that *this* was the designated closet where the songbooks are kept. Then you wouldn't have been such a bother. These must be nice people, though, because they want you to know their names.

Effective small groups consist of more ingredients than name tags. One can sense when many of the elements that make up healthy groups are in place. It is equally obvious when a group has not been aware of the dynamics of group life. People will use terms like *warm, friendly,* and *encouraging* to describe healthy small groups. On the other hand, groups that need help in this area are described as *impersonal, hard to break into,* and *unfriendly.* The people in these groups are not hard to get to know or unfriendly, they only *seem* to be that way in the context of a group. Yet understanding the basics of small group dynamics can transform groups into communities that attract people. Such groups grow because their members are growing relationally. Like a garden with well-fertilized soil, so is the small group which gives attention to the basics of group life.

An Effective Small Group
Bill and Lucy led such a group. Bill was the president of a local business and Lucy did her best to manage a busy household. They responded to a call for someone in their area to open a small Christian growth group. After a couple of months of meetings at the church for training and introduction to group life, they launched out with their small group. On meeting nights, Lucy was always at the door, welcoming each person to their household. To say she had the gift of hospitality was almost an understatement. Each person felt highly valued as he entered into group life at their home. Bill took over the greeting process when people moved into the living room. In the winter, the house filled with the warmth of a fire in the fireplace, fresh-brewed coffee, and usually some baked goodies. In the summer, the sound of the wind flowing through majestic trees made its way into the house, providing a soothing atmosphere for people who needed an oasis.

The group was family. Jim and Betty, though their home was in

Atlanta, found a new "home" in Milwaukee. Their southern friendliness boosted everybody's self-esteem. Betsy often came without her husband. She enriched the group with her depth of wisdom and insight about the Scriptures and how biblical principles apply to life. Her struggle with infertility was deeply painful, yet she shared the pain with her group, gaining strength to continue. Kathy, a single woman, was as bubbly as any person could be. She came to the meeting after stopping at a nursing home to care for her invalid mother after work. She was a dedicated believer with giant buttons all over her coat describing what she thought about Jesus. Nobody where she worked ever had to question where she stood regarding spiritual things. Though she was sometimes quite opinionated, her enthusiasm contributed to lively group worship experiences and discussions.

Dave and Karen were younger than most people in the group. They were newly married and wished to become fully involved in the life of the church. They were directed to this group when it was formed and served as the Bible study leaders. Having the support and encouragement of this group meant so much as they began their married life together. They led the group through many of the biblical discussions, trying not to dominate.

Such is a description of one group—a family, in one sense. Each person felt knit to the other through the common bond of their relationship with Christ and the local church. The group did many things well. In large measure, they had the dynamics which make for an effective group. When you came to meetings, you were warmly greeted, people knew your name, and you knew their names. The house was well lit, so you never had to wonder whether or not you had the right one. The handshakes (and hugs, if you were so inclined) were heartfelt signs of welcome. The chairs were set up to communicate that each person is equally important.

The group existed for a purpose. This was well defined in advance and communicated to people who may have been new. People realized that they would be home by 10:00 P.M. if they needed to be. When they gathered for prayer, they encouraged each person to share requests and pray, but demanded sharing and prayer of no one. They collectively carried the struggles of everyday life and celebrated joys together. But this community didn't happen by accident. In the training of the leaders and the group, they became aware of those vital elements which bond a group together.

Essential Elements of a Small Group

Dr. Russell D. Robinson, in his book *Dynamics of Group Leadership* (Omni Book Co., 1979) describes four essential elements which are the minimum requirements for the formation of any stable group. They are acceptance, communication, structure, and purpose. Acceptance is necessary for people to feel respected, recognized, and valued. They find security in groups that breed acceptance. They trust and are trusted. Some system of communication is also vital. This can be described as the bloodstream of the group. Values, beliefs, opinions, and frustrations are carried by this system. A structure or organization is also important for the group. Even groups that pride themselves on being flexible have some form of structure, even if it is implicit. Control and freedom must be exercised through this structure. The group must also work for a common goal or purpose which must be understood by the group for best effectiveness.

To these four ingredients we may add a few more for maximum effectiveness of a small group. Recognition of people's backgrounds greatly enhances the life of a group. In the one described above, Bill had a tremendous practical sense when it came to financial matters. As such, he could be called upon to aid those who had problems or needed advice regarding money. Betsy had spent many hours digging in the Scriptures. Her insight helped the group navigate through difficult theological questions.

Developing cohesion, or unity, is not only helpful for group life but a command from Jesus to follow. Too often petty squabbles explode into major rifts in groups which do not work at growing together. Finally, standards for procedures and evaluation can aid the group to do self-examination for gauging its effectiveness. Few groups simply "happen" to be dynamic. Most groups that are considered effective, vibrant entities have worked hard at putting it all together. The ingredients are in place to make it effective.

Bill and Lucy's group had many things going for it. They had given attention to many of these concerns. At one point, the group participated in a city-wide evangelistic effort. This activity gave the group a new focus. The members had been knit together in loving and caring relationships. Now they were beginning to look outside of themselves for the sake of those who had not yet responded in faith and obedience to Christ. The church offered training to enable the group to be more effective in its outreach. The group trained together to reach out; they prayed together for those whom they targeted to be invited to the outreach. They studied together to understand the necessity of evangelism and how they could explain their own faith effectively. The task of outreach further bonded the group together. When the appointed time for outreach came, they rejoiced together to see what God had done through their efforts.

The group went on to form a new church with other groups in the area, with the encouragement of the sponsoring church. Bill and Lucy, not surprisingly, opened their home on Sunday nights for this fledgling church. It grew to over 800 people after 10 years. Much of the success of that church is attributed to people in groups such as Bill and Lucy's, groups in which people can learn what it means to live in true community, love, and unity. These groups model what the church is supposed to be.

Bill and Lucy's group eventually stopped meeting. Each group has its own life cycle. The people did not stop growing, however. They simply shifted to new relationships, new endeavors to enable the church to grow strong. New groups formed and are showing people how to continue living life in fellowship with others in the body of Christ.

A Small Group Failure

When groups are functioning with maximum effectiveness the dynamics of the group are usually very well attended to. If a group tends to be lifeless, listless, or useless, it is not hard to pinpoint the problem. Take the case of Bob's group. He was often on the phone with the pastor in charge of his small group to complain about the "lack of response" and "criticism" from the people in his group. The pastor had occasionally attended meetings and found friendliness and openness among most of the people. In probing more deeply, he uncovered a basic unwillingness on the part of the leader to openly discuss his own frustrations with the group although members probably would have been accepting of his concerns and very willing to change. The leader's basic inability to open up and model transparency in communication stifled the group. As a result, the group disbanded and the leader, in bitterness and anger, still holds a grudge against the people in his group for not acting the way he wanted (even though he never communicated his needs). In this case, it was easy to spot the leader's lack of communication that doomed the group.

Looking Ahead
Such failures are needless tragedies. Every group can improve its effectiveness through giving attention to developing seven basic group dynamic areas: acceptance, purpose, communication, structure, backgrounds, cohesion, and standards. This book treats each area in detail, giving practical advice for small group leaders and participants to enhance group life. We also will look at the normal life cycle of a group to understand each of the different stages. Consequently, a group leader will not be surprised when a new group encounters initial uneasiness with one another or when a more established group begins to venture into the uncharted waters of vulnerability. The goal in this process is not simply to make groups better. Rather, it is to provide an environment for the church to be a model of wholeness and community for the world to see.

Review and Reflection
1. What are the ingredients that have made you feel welcome and accepted in a group?
2. Why is it important to know the patterns of communication that are to be followed for a group? How will people feel if they do not know such procedures?
3. What characteristics did Bill and Lucy have that made them so effective?
4. Why would somebody like Betsy, who struggled with infertility, share that with a small group?
5. How can knowing someone's background help in developing group life?
6. What questions can you think of at this stage that could be used to evaluate the effectiveness of a group?

TWO

THE SMALL GROUP DYNAMICS GRID

"Now learn this lesson from the fig tree: As soon as its twigs get tender and its leaves come out, you know that summer is near. Even so, when you see these things happening, you know that is is near, right at the door. I tell you the truth, this generation will certainly not pass away until all these things have happened. Heaven and earth will pass away, but My words will never pass away" (Mark 13:28-31).

Jesus gave the teachers of the Law the "big picture." In the same way, we need to get the big picture if we want to maximize the effectiveness of our groups. To this end, it is helpful to examine the way the elements of small group dynamics relate to one another graphically. A grid or diagram shows the interplay between the elements that make for healthy small groups.

Task vs. Relationship
Small groups are either primarily task oriented or relationship oriented. These two types of groups form two ends of the spectrum

when looking at small group ministry. On the side of relationships, we hope to develop an atmosphere of caring, sharing, having an opportunity for expression of love and concern. All that we are and all that another person is contributes to the overall effectiveness of building relationships. It is difficult to conceive of any group that wouldn't have some emphasis on building relationships. The interaction between believers is not only mandated by the Scriptures but also is healthy and therapeutic.

Types of Groups

Task		Relationship

On the other side of the spectrum is the emphasis on fulfilling the task. The task can vary from simply studying the Scriptures together to contacting every house in a neighborhood in an evangelistic effort. Just as it is difficult to conceive of any group not having some emphasis on relationships, so also every group has some task to accomplish, even if it is not stated.

When we look at the predominant flavor of a small group, we notice that there is a tendency to focus more on tasks or on relationships. This is not to say that an emphasis either way is wrong; it is just the way the group operates.

What we often call "committees" fit into the category of task groups with specific functions. One of the committees within the couples ministry at Elmbrook Church is the Special Events Committee. This group meets many times each year to plan, strategize, and bring to fruition ideas that will lead to a greater involvement of couples in the ministry. The group is primarily task oriented. They have the job of planning retreats, Valentine dinners, and social involvement projects; but they also build some relationships within that group.

Focus on God or People
There is another way of looking at small group relationships. Groups may focus primarily on people-to-people involvement. Or

they may emphasize a people-to-God relationship. In other words, the focus might be different, depending on the type of group that is desired. A group that focuses more exclusively on people will be geared either in the direction of greater fellowship, caring, and sharing with one another or in the area of service to one another. Thus, a practical task that is directed toward another person may be in the area of social involvement. An example is Habitat for Humanity, which seeks to build homes to benefit people who are on the lower end of the economic spectrum. The task, which is most important, is to build a low-cost house. Relationships may be strengthened, although relationship building is not the primary goal. Nevertheless, it is a people-to-people focus.

On the other side of the spectrum is a focus on God. While it may seem to indicate worship, that is only one part of this focus. Certainly, the relational aspect of focusing on God includes adoration and worship. However, if we are learning about God—that is, studying the Scriptures together to find out about Him—we are able to discern that God has tasks for us to do and we need to find out what they are. This process is also a part of focusing upon God.

Putting the Grid in Perspective
In examining the distinctions between a focus on God and a focus on people and relationship vs. task group, we can see that these are interrelated. They form a grid that can be used as a tool for evaluating the groups of which we are a part. We then can discern where the different elements of our small groups rest on this grid. In doing so, we will understand why certain elements of small group dynamics are more important than others, depending on the type of group it is.

Let us look at different events that groups may schedule on a regular basis in order to see how they relate to the small group ministries grid. The first, and perhaps most common event, is fellowship—talking with one another, caring for one another, just simply sharing our lives with one another. Identifying where this event is on the grid is not difficult; it is on the side of focusing on people, toward relationships. The group is not unbalanced; people are exercising an appropriate function for that particular group.

Another event that occurs in small groups is service. This could

SMALL GROUP DYNAMICS GRID

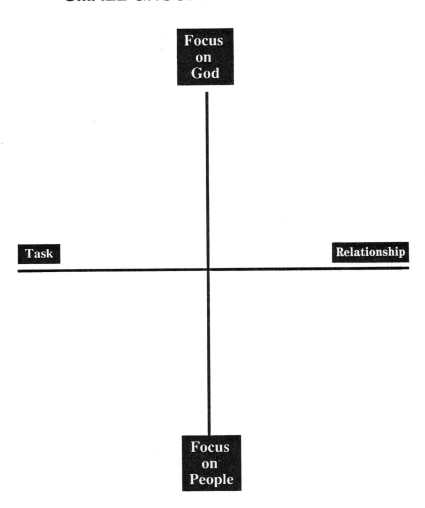

SMALL GROUP DYNAMICS GRID

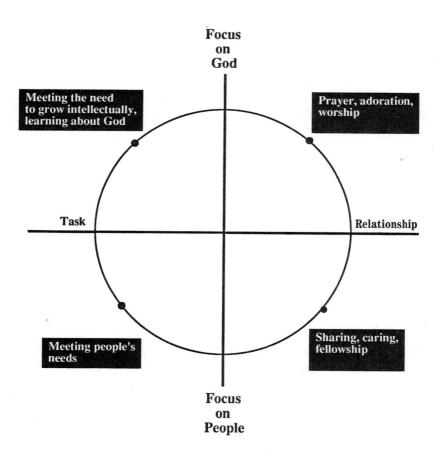

21

be as simple as providing a meal for someone in need. Or it could be a more complicated task, such as coordinating and participating in the building of houses for needy people. The task is most important in this kind of project. The focus is to help another person, but relationship building is not in the forefront. Again, it is not improper for a group to have this kind of focus as long as it is discerned ahead of time as being a legitimate part of the group's function.

Most small groups in the Christian community do some kind of Bible study. In some groups that focus primarily on tasks, the Bible study may a brief devotional. But even groups that emphasize Bible study may be task focused with the aim of gaining insight. Although it may have a result of focusing on people, the focus is primarily on God. What has God said to us? How can I be godly? The task may be finding out what kind of a spiritual gift I might have or just simply finding out what else I must know about God in order to live more in the light of His goodness. This kind of emphasis on Bible study — discerning what God wants — is primarily task oriented and a focusing on God.

Another emphasis that we see in some groups is worship. It is not difficult to discern at this point that worship emphasizes focusing on God, particularly our personal relationship with God. To have a relationship with God requires us to spend time in addressing Him and in giving thanks to Him. Groups that have this emphasis as part of their overall experience will at this point be focusing on God and on relationships.

This summary completes the small group dynamics grid. There are other points that we could add to the overall picture, but the grid itself is complete.

It is possible to place any event or function of a group on this grid. It is helpful for group leaders, then, to begin to evaluate the style, emphasis, or bent of the group. Does it have a predominant tendency to focus on relationships as opposed to tasks? Is there more of a focus on God or on people? This is not to say that any focus is right or wrong. We must simply recognize that we should evaluate the focus and decide whether it is in line with the stated purposes and goals of the small group.

Elements of Small Group Dynamics and the Grid

Now let us consider where the different small group dynamic elements fit in the grid, starting with *acceptance*. If we are trying to build a group that is accepting of one another, it is not difficult to see that the focus is on relationships. We need not accept another person in order to work alongside him to accomplish a task. However, if we are to build a relationship with another person, there must be some recognition of the value of that person and acceptance of his background, gifts, and abilities.

Even his quirks must be accepted. This fact is not only true in focusing on people, but also in focusing on God Himself. God has chosen through Christ to accept us, allowing us to respond in a humble attitude of worship toward God. Worshiping God is an acceptance of God. The salvation that we enjoy is God's acceptance of us.

On the other hand, if we look at the *purposes* that need to be established for the group, we lean toward the idea of task. Even if the purpose is to provide fellowship, the purpose in and of itself is a task that needs to be accomplished. Though it will be expanded upon later, every group needs to have an understandable set of purposes. The purpose, of course, can be focused on people — either in what we will do for people or with them. Or the focus can be on God — what we will do in response to His desires or what we will discern of God. In either case, the purpose is a task that needs to be accomplished. To have a stated goal of spending one hour in Bible study each week is to say we want to focus on God to learn about him and how we are to respond. But it is a Godward focus even though there is a task to be accomplished.

If we look at people's *backgrounds* and how they relate to a small group, we most often find that we are focusing on how people relate to one another. Whether they relate well often depends on their backgrounds. The same is true in relating to God. I know of a number of people who have difficulty relating to God because their own fathers fell desperately short of what God intended a father to be. Thus, when they think of God as Father, their backgrounds have skewed any appropriate vision into something grotesque, seriously affecting their worship.

On the other side of the grid are *standards and procedures*.

SMALL GROUP DYNAMICS GRID

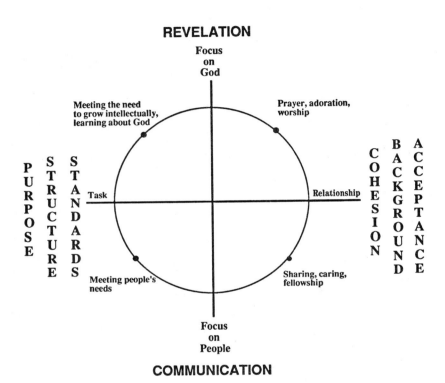

They address how we go about the task that we are to accomplish. The emphasis is on how to, rather than on to whom. Thus we have certain procedures we follow when we study the Bible and focus on God. We also follow certain procedures when we look at how we relate to one another and how we care about and share with each other.

In addition, we may also need to develop a sense of unity called *cohesion*. Groups that are knit together enjoy brotherly love and affection. They may be bound together just with a common purpose, but the relationship is built because of this cohesion.

Cohesion is that vague element that says we are not just a group of disparate individuals, but we are vitally linked to one another. Cohesion relates to the individual's relationship with either another person or with God Himself. God has taken the initiative to make us one with Him. It goes beyond the idea of acceptance to the additional step of being linked in a familial relationship with God.

Another important aspect of group dynamics, though this time on the side of the task emphasis, is the area of *structure*. Structure is concerned most of all with providing limits to both protect and enhance the group. Structure allows the group to carry out its tasks within defined limits. Thus it is most concerned with the tasks at hand.

There are two additional parts of the small group dynamics puzzle that need to be placed on the grid. The first is the area of communication. Communication as used here focuses on people to people interaction. The way people gain a sense of understanding is through communication, be it verbal or nonverbal. Whether the group is going to get on with the task or be knit in closer relationship with one another, communication is vital. Thus, at least as far as the small group dynamics grid is concerned, it is placed on the people end of the spectrum.

The flipside is what we call revelation. It is concerned with the interaction between a holy God and a fallen human race. If there is no communication from God that is revelation, then there is no way we can respond to Him. Thus, any focusing on God depends on revelation. This element distinguishes the Christian small group from all others. Revelation from God is acknowledged as essential for life just as communication between people is essential for our lives. Even our worship depends on God's revelation to us. He shows us Himself, and we respond accordingly to that revelation. This is not to say that we don't communicate with God. We do. But it is always in response to revelation from God.

When viewed as a whole, the small group dynamics grid is complete. We will see that whether a group focuses on relationships or tasks, or whether it is primarily geared toward relating to God or people, small group dynamics contribute to the overall well-being of a group. This fact leads to a corollary to our understanding of the small group dynamics grid.

Using the Grid
The type of group we seek to establish highlights the relative importance of these elements of small group dynamics. If, according to its purpose, a small group wants to focus on building relationships — that is, fellowship, sharing, and caring — it is not difficult to see that the most important aspects of small group dynamics are the development of acceptance, understanding of backgrounds, and the development of cohesion among the group members. Of course, vitally linked to these dynamics are good communication patterns. Of lesser importance are standards and procedures, a defined purpose, and structures. Again, this is not to say that these areas aren't important. Rather, it is more important for a group focusing on friendliness, sharing, and caring, and concern for one another to major on the small group dynamics pieces that are on the relationship side of the grid.

Likewise, if a group is gathered around a task of sponsoring a couples' retreat in the future, determining methods, standards, a stated goal, and a structure within which they will reach that stated goal is of utmost importance. Acceptance of one another, a discerning of people's backgrounds, and a sense of cohesion is not nearly as important. At any given time within a group's life or a group meeting, small group leaders should be able to discern where that group resides on the grid. Most groups jump around. At one point in an evening there will be a tremendous focus on personal relationships, at another point there is worship. At another point there is a sense of discerning what God has to say to them, and at another point they talk about how they can practically care for an area of need that exists within the group or the community.

My recommendation, which is developed more thoroughly in chapter 4, is to plan an equal balance between the four quadrants of the grid. We can move around within the grid; but a balanced view of the four provides for a balanced group. There is a need for task groups, there is a need for groups that focus exclusively on fellowship, there is a need for groups that exist exclusively for prayer or Bible study. But a full-orbed small group program will offer a balance of these functions.

Review and Reflection

1. What is the primary emphasis in your small group or in a group of which you are aware? Can you locate this emphasis on the small group dynamics grid?
2. In what way does worship use both revelation and communication? Do you agree with the statement that worship and communication depend on revelation? Why or why not?
3. How can communication be so important for both fulfilling tasks and developing relationships?
4. In what ways are standards, structures, and purposes most important for a task group, e.g., one that needs to put together a church building proposal?
5. Why are such elements as an atmosphere of acceptance, a sense of cohesion, and an understanding of people's backgrounds most important in developing deep, enriching relationships?
6. How can you use the small group dynamics grid to evaluate groups?

THREE

AN ATMOSPHERE
OF ACCEPTANCE

Accept one another, then just as Christ accepted you, in order to bring praise to God (Romans 15:7).

It would be hard to claim that anything carries more importance than establishing an atmosphere of acceptance in a small group. Groups which are described as cliquish, closed, or unfriendly have not dealt with this issue. The Scriptures give us the important command: "Accept one another, then, just as Christ accepted you, in order to bring praise to God" (Romans 15:7). We are confronted with the fact that Christ's actions of absolute acceptance in response to our faith provide the model for the church. This instruction must not be overlooked by our groups, which are a snapshot of the church at large. There are certainly times when groups may by definition target a certain group of people such as singles, senior citizens, or couples. But even within those groups, everyone needs to feel the warmth of acceptance.

SMALL GROUP DYNAMICS GRID

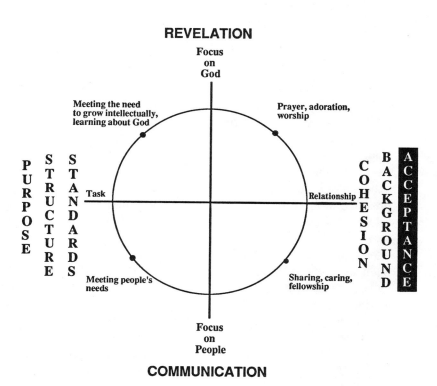

Importance for the Group

Building Self-Esteem

Most psychologists today tell us of the wide-ranging difficulties people have in simply accepting themselves for who they are. Because of widespread physical and emotional abuse in families, as well as the pervasive problems people have after being raised in other dysfunctional family situations, many are crying out for a place that can be a haven for healing these deep hurts. This place does not have to be a therapy group, although they are very valuable. A group of believers who freely accept whom the Lord brings to their door can be very helpful.

People within these groups experience the healing of being loved simply because they are there and not because they necessarily have something to offer the group or carry some special status. Others affirm them simply because they recognize the value of their presence within the group. People who are struggling with low self-esteem can venture out to try things within a small group which they would never do in their usual settings. The encouragement offered in such groups plants seeds of new ambitions and creativity. Such ambition then sprouts experimentations in using gifts and tackling challenges. The group can lovingly steer this creativity to maximize the person's gifts and talents.

So much depends on the leaders when it comes to establishing an accepting group. Take Jim and Jan, for instance. Their group seemed to attract the walking wounded. So many had deep personal and emotional problems. It was not difficult to detect why Jim and Jan were so successful in reaching these people. When you walked into their home, the aroma of love enveloped you and would not let you go. You could not miss it. They were so delighted in your presence that you wished you could move in right then and there! Gradually these fragile people grew to become helpers and encouragers themselves rather than the helped and encouraged. They owe Jim and Jan for their healing efforts. Jim and Jan know what it is to accept others just as Christ has accepted them.

Incorporation of New People

Assimilating new people is accentuated when groups know how to be accepting. We all have heard the negative side to this situation.

People try to find a group (or church) and return to say how cold and unfriendly a group is. Few people determine in advance to be unfriendly. But many groups inadvertantly maintain a standoffish attitude. If they had followed some simple guidelines, they would be able to transform their atmosphere from cold to warm, aloof to open.

Recently I went into a group and was surprised at how I was greeted. Even though I was their pastor, I was amazed how insecure I felt going into a group I hadn't been to for some time. I felt like a newcomer to the group. I was acknowledged as being there, but not much else happened to make me feel welcome. It was not that these leaders were unfriendly, only that they assumed that their group was accepting, warm, and open to new people. My experience, however, was not that way. As I talk with people who are new to the church, I am struck by their reticence of visiting one of our groups. I know they could attend certain groups which bend over backwards to incorporate the newcomer, making him or her feel most welcome.

Openness for Sharing
Len, a key leader within a small group, related the story about a men's prayer breakfast that his small group sponsored. Usually both men and women, single or married, attended group meetings. But for this morning, the time was set aside just for the men to meet and pray. One of the men gave a riveting confession about an area of life he had been struggling with for years. He knew it was not in line with what God had for him, yet he continued to have problems. Soon, in the confines of that small group of men, others shared their own difficulties and the ways they were drawing upon God's strength to deal decisively with the issues. Len, who was part of that meeting, spoke of the amazing openness that the men had in speaking of such personal issues. Such transparency is a rarity in the world and, sadly, in many churches today. The group's ability to accept each individual allowed the environment to be fertile for such sharing.

Preserving Group Unity
Few would question the importance of an atmosphere of acceptance in preserving group unity. It is obvious that we should receive

others regardless of their "peculiar" tendencies. (We, of course, are not peculiar at all, are we?) But we all have certain prejudices that militate against developing unity. We feel most drawn to those like ourselves. The oddball gets scrutinized closely to see if he or she will fit in with the group.

The model we should follow comes from Jesus' ministry. His disciples were a small group. They certainly had much in common. For example, they were all from Jewish descent and the same area of the country. But even though they had certain shared qualities, they did not always model an accepting and forgiving attitude. The small group, called the Twelve in the New Testament, had people like James and John, the sons of Zebedee. They requested the highest standing within the group: "Let one of us sit at your right and the other at your left in your glory," was their expressed desire (Mark 10:35-45). In other words, "We're the greatest of this small group." It is no wonder that the rest of the disciples became indignant. Jesus used this episode to give a teaching on group unity. Unity depends on acceptance, and the mark of acceptance is service. The finest leader of any small group, Jesus, used Himself as the example of the servant. People who freely accept one another serve one another.

Audrey talked too much about herself and her problems when she attended the small group she wished to join. She was a handful for the leaders of that group. This situation could have threatened the existence of the group and Audrey's well-being. If the leaders allowed her to monopolize the conversation, then others would resent the amount of time she took. If they cut her off, she might leave. Years later, she still has problems. But her life has stabilized, and she is a vital part of the group and a valuable link in the starting of a new church. Her group gave her the chance to talk when she first became a part of them. But gradually they dealt with her firmly, directing her to consider others just as important as herself. She listened more and prayed more for other people. Acceptance of her allowed for unity; her recognition of the need of unity within the group as a whole, i.e., the voluntary reduction of the amount of time she took for the sake of others, allowed her to show acceptance of the group.

Fulfilling Scripture

Perhaps the demands of Scripture give us the most compelling reasons for maintaining an atmosphere of acceptance. Examining each of the "one another" commands reveals the lengths to which we must go in developing mutual regard for each other.

> *Accept One Another.* "Accept one another, then, just as Christ accepted you, in order to bring praise to God (Romans 15:7).

There is little doubt of the applicability of this verse to our study. It is the basis for what we do in small group ministry. But let us not allow the obvious to simply massage the brain cells into a simple nod of assent. The great apostle Paul was writing to Jews who had a difficult time accepting Gentiles and Gentiles who had difficulty receiving Jews. Paul's whole point in Romans 9–11, and again picked up here in Romans 15, is to show the greatness of God in making Jews and Gentiles one in Christ. Allowing both to be linked together is the gift of God for which He should be praised. God has not said simply that Jewish and Gentile people should act nicely toward each other as if it were a divine suggestion. The deep chasm which separated the two groups has now been totally demolished. The spiritual barrenness of the Gentiles has been enriched by Christ's work. The spiritual haughtiness of the Jewish people has been replaced by gratitude for God's working in history to include the Gentiles. Gentiles must no longer live in that barrenness but can be grateful for God's inclusion of them in His kingdom.

This is wonderful theology. But how does it affect our small groups? There is no small group that I can think of that hasn't had to wrestle with issues of people's personal backgrounds and attitudes toward one another. One can liken it to the reality after the honeymoon stops. Initially stars emanate from the eyes of a newly married couple as they march down the aisle toward marital bliss. They march off to their honeymoon hideaway on cloud nine; months later they march out of the house, both wondering why the person they married has changed into a mere mortal.

Small groups carry a similar life pattern. Initially, the energy of the group is electrifying. Everyone has a sense of expectancy as they meet and find out about one another. A few months later they realize how weird some of the people really are. A dose of acceptance applied at that moment transforms the group from the mediocrity of surface relationships to the depth of caring necessary for healthy group life. A transformation takes place when a group gets serious about this command.

Greet One Another. "Greet one another with a holy kiss. All the churches of Christ send greetings" (Romans 16:16).

Very few people take this command literally. And most are glad they don't. A kiss was the culturally accepted greeting at that time and location. Few would deny the importance of the principle, however. A greeting is the fundamental recognition of personhood; you matter if you are greeted. How many of us are thrilled down to our toes when we receive a personal letter from one we care about deeply? A letter, such as the one Paul wrote to the Roman church, was a way of sending a greeting; a kiss was a way of translating that greeting into a personal encounter.

A few years ago, I attended a small group where I knew the leaders quite well. Yet I knew almost nobody else. I felt like an absolute newcomer to the group (which I was!). Even though I was in charge of the ministry to small groups, I still felt very uncomfortable when I walked into that house. The leaders greeted me, but no one else did. I was introduced as the pastor of the ministry, and my name was given to the group. But I learned no one else's name through that encounter. The greeting, in essence, went one way. They knew who I was, but I did not have a clue as to who they were. That sense of uneasiness that came from not being greeted and acknowledged individually pervaded the meeting from my perspective. It was possible to overcome that situation, but the experience drove home the issue of how important a greeting was.

Today there are socially accepted greetings that are desperately important for a small group to employ. Hugs and kisses in many church cultures in the United States, for instance, are not acceptable for newcomers. If you are going to hug the stuffing out of someone, you better know for sure that he or she is comfortable with that gesture. The two most important acts within the cultures of most churches are the handshake and the exchange of names.

Leaders of groups can sit on the sidelines to see whether their group members are following the biblical command to greet one another. For most group leaders, this exercise would be an eye-opening experience.

Bear with one another. "Be completely humble and gentle; be patient, bearing with one another in love" (Ephesians 4:2).

The operative injunction here is to bear with one another in love. This is long-term patience. Some people are like finger nails on a blackboard. Not only are they irritating; but the longer you deal with them, the harder they are to take. The church has difficult people within it. Some are naturally drawn to one another like magnets; others are repelled like magnets turned the wrong way. But the church models unity when we bear with one another, accepting another's strangeness as an important growth tool God uses in our lives. That doesn't mean we don't occasionally have to discuss disagreements and opposing opinions. We choose within those disagreements to agree that we are united in Christ.

Linked with this command is the need for gentleness and humility. Autocratic, domineering people model acceptance poorly. They haven't found the key of humility and gentleness which unlocks the hearts of other people. After all, an assertion of superiority seldom breeds warmth. Gentleness has been described as power under control. How appropriate this description is for group life. The power to destroy and build up resides within each person of a small group. This power used wrongly will break up a group. Even a few words inappropriately spoken can take months to heal. Healing, edifying words, however, can bring wholeness. The power of the tongue used indiscriminately brings destruction; that same power, used under control, brings life. We all know those who seem to have the ability to destroy with the tongue. They have not learned the lesson of Ephesians 4:2. Let it not pass by us.

Be kind and compassionate to one another. "Be kind and compassionate to one another, forgiving each other, just as in Christ God forgave you" (Ephesians 4:32).

Do you remember the bumper sticker that read PBPGINFWMY? The letters stand for: Please Be Patient, God Is Not Finished With Me Yet. While this attitude should not be an excuse for bad driving, it should be a mark of a small group. Kindness and compassion bring freedom for the downcast. Recently a woman remarked, "One reason I continue coming to this church is that the people deal kindly with those in need and who are struggling with personal issues." Small groups — the picture of the "church-at-small" in distinction from the "church-at-large" — can offer the same environment. People with personal needs do not need judging but warm caring.

At a leaders' meeting, one person commented on a situation which developed within his group. It seems that one member was using the group as a source for business customers. The group responded to this person's appeals and provided some income for his business. A second person came into the group, moved into the same line of work, and then realized that the small group was all "tapped out" and would not yield any more money. A rift developed between the two participants in the group. The second person was angry at the first for "stealing" all of his customers. In the end the second person would not attend if the first person were there. In a word, the situation was a mess.

The group leader was totally unaware of the situation because it was happening behind the scenes. Finally, when he was able to discern what was going on, it was obvious that the leader had to help these two people learn about compassion, kindness, and forgiveness. After making it clear that the group was not to be viewed as a source of customers, the leader next had to foster a forgiving attitude within the two people. This was not easy but it needed to be done for the sake of the group. The warmth of a caring atmosphere is what was needed most, not the air of competition.

Be devoted to and honor one another. "Be devoted to one another in brotherly love. Honor one another above yourselves" (Romans 12:10).

Christians must begin to live together as part of a new, healthy family. The link between believers is a family tie, joined together by the free act of God the Father in adopting us into His family. This new attitude of devotion markedly contrasts situations of the many people who have grown up in unhealthy, dysfunctional families, who long for the stability of a new family. Then, as we link honor to devotion, people are built up by seeing others not only care, but visibly give preference to others. All this is accomplished by recognizing the way God has gifted others. Believers honor one another by allowing gifts to be exercised and affirming them in that employment of gifts.

Confess sins to and pray for one another. "Therefore, confess your sins to each other and pray for each other so that you may be healed. The prayer of a righteous man is powerful and effective" (James 5:16).

Scripture links two commands together: confess and pray. Groups should have time for admission of struggles and hurts. Handled in the appropriate way, through prayer and care, affirmation and acceptance are engendered.

Margaret, struggling with cancer, called her small group together for prayer. Her desire was to live faithfully before God and in community with others. The group, with splendid affirmation, surrounded her one evening with fervent prayer, gentle touch, and honoring testimony. She faced decisions, fears, worries, weakness. Her own testimony—confession, if you will—of helplessness traveled deep into the hearts of the people around her. The group enriched her life; she enriched theirs. But it took an affirmation of weakness and need before the warmth of caring and fellowship could flow. After nearly two hours of sharing testimony, Scripture, and prayer, the group dispersed. But they did not leave until they had given Margaret what she had asked for. Oh, that we might value one another's prayers! Then we may seriously pray ourselves. Such prayer for one another cannot help but breed an accepting, caring group.

Stir up one another. "And let us consider how we may spur one another on toward love and good deeds" (Hebrews 10:24).

John and Mary, group leaders, received an appeal one day. The caller asked them to write an encouraging letter to a man who was receiving mail criticizing the exercise of his gift. In short, the man, who was gifted in music, was severely criticized for his choice of musical styles, even to the point of questioning his ability to lead in worship. John and Mary, who had the gift of encouragement, were urged to exercise that gift in writing a letter. The caller spurred them on to exercise their own gift. Then, through the use of their gift, they could spur another person on to actively use his gift. Through one phone call asking John and Mary to exercise their gift, many benefited.

Spurring one another on to love and good deeds requires the group leader to keep several points in mind. First of all, the leader needs to keep his or her eyes open to the areas and levels of giftedness in different individuals. Secondly, the group leader must note the types of needs that group members have. Are they in need of encouragement? Are they in need of teaching? Is there an opportunity to help in some very practical way?

Third, a leader must match need with gift. This point is where many people become frustrated. Unfortunately, leaders tend to use one mode of operation when there are needs: They ask for volunteers. Volunteerism may be on the rise nationally, but finding volunteers for tasks in the church is a poor way of meeting needs. Linking gift with need through personal contact is the best method for encouraging people to actively use their gifts. Group leaders must face the fact that if they want to involve someone in meeting a need, they should contact him in person, identifying both the need and the reason they think that person is gifted to meet the need.

Marks of a Healthy Group
The above discussion presents a sense of what is healthy and helpful for a group. First of all, when you walk into a group that is accepting, you are warmly greeted and affirmed simply because you chose to put aside other activities to be with the group. This acceptance certainly is important for newcomers. But it is no less important for long-standing group members. We should not assume that a person's commitment level to a group (or enjoyment level, for that matter) will remain constant throughout the time he identifies with the group. A healthy, hearty greeting and affirmation for everyone

helps maintain interest in the group.

A second mark of a healthy group is joy. A group that truly accepts each other is a joyful group. Laughter and smiles characterize the meetings. Group members are not easily perturbed by the actions of others. Instead, they model scriptural patience and forbearance. When difficult issues come up, they listen to each other, avoiding simplistic answers. They really focus on one another's needs. They enjoy one another.

Bill and Marge were leaders of a couples' group. But for four weeks, the group met with several hundred other people for a time of worship, teaching, and encouragement. Consequently, the group was not functioning as a unit for a month. At the end of that month, members of their group testified about how they missed getting together with one another. They couldn't wait for the large group emphasis to end so they could get back with one another, rekindling relationships. They cared for each other so much that they longed for each other. Joy characterized their lives together.

A third mark of a well-maintained group is the ability to assimilate newcomers. New people are not easily integrated into the life of the group unless they feel accepted and wanted. The group that sincerely cares for all, whether they are members or not, is practicing this important element of acceptance.

Guidelines for Leaders

The single most important tip for the leader is to model acceptance. Every person should be able to do so; but it is most important for the leader, who should continually pray about his matter. Acceptance is an attitude of the heart that leads to actions enhancing a sense of acceptance. So when we talk of modeling, we are not talking about outward appearances only, that is, the things we do to communicate acceptance. Rather, we must focus on our inner thoughts, asking for the same attitude as God has for us.

This fact does not mean we don't act. We must. The leader ought to be the first to extend a hand of greeting to people. She should lead in finding out about other people's backgrounds, hobbies, desires, and goals. She can be the mark for which other group members shoot.

Kathy is one of those who sets a high mark. Rarely does a day go by when she has not contacted someone from the group to see how that person is doing. She constantly talks to newcomers to make them feel welcome. She is the epitome of acceptance; her care and concern flow from her countenance. People are drawn to her because they feel safe around her. It is not difficult to understand why that group is full. The house is jammed with people who respond well to Kathy's inviting, joyful attitude.

The group leader can also talk about the atmosphere with the group. In essence, the group can evaluate itself in this most crucial area. Questions like the following can aid evaluation: How can we be sensitive to people's needs? What can we do to make newcomers feel safe and welcome? How joyful a group are we? What can we do to communicate acceptance to each other more effectively?

In short, the leader can study the "one another" commands in the New Testament to help himself gain the proper view of how we should relate to one another. Studying these commands in the group is even more helpful. But studying does not insure action. Actions, application of the Word, is of utmost importance as we seek to affirm the value and status of other individuals.

Discussion Starters

The following discussion starter questions may be helpful in developing openness and acceptance within a group. Often they are used in conjunction with people introducing themselves. Groups that use these questions have raved about their effectiveness. But not all questions are appropriate for each group, so be selective.

1. Share a funny thing that happened to you when you were a child.
2. Talk about someone whom you really respect and admire. Tell why.
3. Are you really listening? What did you hear the last person say?
4. Complete this statement: Something I really appreciate is _____.
5. How do you show love for the people in your family?
6. Share a time when you felt left out.
7. Who has helped you most in your life? How?
8. Tell about your favorite holiday and why you think it is special.

9. Tell about a time when you felt depressed.
10. How would you describe your family to someone else?
11. Complete this statement: The most patient member of my family is _____.
12. Who do you think is the most loving member of your family? Why?
13. What worries you most?
14. Talk about a time when you really had fun with your family.
15. With whom in your family do you feel you can communicate best? Why?
16. How do you feel when you know that you have upset someone in your family.
17. Share a frustration that you have.
18. Tell about something that really upsets you.
19. Complete this statement: Someone I can always trust is _____.
20. Name three things that make your family happy.
21. Tell about a time when you felt guilty.
22. If you were asked to draw a picture of something to symbolize the members of your family, what would you draw for each one?
23. Share a time when you were really frightened.
24. Share one of your strengths and one of your weaknesses.
25. Think of something nice that someone in your family has done and express your appreciation.
26. Complete the statement: The thing that we disagree the most about in our family is _____.
27. What is the best thing for you to do when you feel yourself becoming angry?
28. Tell about a dream that you remember.
29. Share a concern that you have for one of your family members.
30. To whom can you tell your deepest secret? Why?
31. How do you think the person across from you would describe you to someone else?
32. Say something about marriage.
33. Complete this statement: My greatest goal in life is _____.
34. What makes you feel proud?
35. How do you act when you are angry?
36. Describe your mother in three words.

37. How do you feel about the rules in your family?
38. Give your description of an ideal family.
39. Describe a fantastic vacation for you and your family.
40. Describe your father in three words.
41. What family holiday experience has left pleasant memories?
42. Complete this statement: What I like about my parents is _____.
43. What freedom do you value the most?
44. Give an imaginary gift to each member of your family (something you think they would really like).
45. How would you like to change your family to make it better?
46. What is the best way for someone to show you love?
47. Complete this statement: Something I really need from my family is _____.
48. Tell about a time when you felt ashamed.
49. Complete this statement: What I would like my children to inherit from me is _____.
50. Say something about arguing.
51. If someone nags you, how does it make you feel?
52. When you feel sad, what is the best thing someone can do for you?
53. Tell about a family (or a person) that you know that seems happy.
54. With whom in your family do you have the most difficulty communicating? Why?
55. Think about the members of your family, and describe each person in one word.
56. Complete this statement: My favorite time of the day is _____.
57. Who do you think is the most helpful member of your family? Why?
58. Complete this statement: If our family inherited a million dollars, I would like for us to _____.
59. Say something about nagging.
60. Talk about your temper and what you do when you lose it.
61. What do you think about sarcastic remarks?
62. Who do you think is the most generous member of your family? Why?

63. Tell about your favorite TV show and why you like it.
64. Who in your family has the best sense of humor?
65. Talk about the best day of this past week.
66. What is likely to cause you to blow up?
67. Tell about something you would like to accomplish in the coming year.
68. Share a time when you felt lonely.
69. Name something you enjoy doing with your family.

Review and Reflection
1. In what ways does God show His acceptance of us? What parallels can you identify for how we can be accepting of others?
2. Paint a verbal picture of a group that is not very accepting. What would you see in such a group?
3. With which of the "one another" commands did you most identify? How would you apply this command in your own situation?
4. In evaluating your group, when was there a great deal of acceptance being shown? When was there a lack of acceptance?
5. What preparations can be made ahead of time so that a group will be able to show acceptance to one another?
6. What effects do the following have on building an atmosphere of acceptance: name tags, refreshments, seating arrangements, arguments?

Four

Groups with Purpose

Do you not know that in a race all the runners run, but only one gets the prize? Run in such a way as to get the prize (1 Corinthians 9:24).

"Where there is no vision, the people perish," Solomon wrote (Proverbs 29:18, KJV). He knew the importance of providing a goal—a purpose, something to reach for—for God's people. It is likewise true for groups. There must be some reason for being, some purpose, some stated goal.

Victor Frankl, in his reflection on the existence of those in concentration camps, knew the importance of hope. Prisoners who lost that sense of purpose and hope declined very quickly and died. Those who were able to maintain hope in the midst of horrid circumstances were able to survive. Without hope, there is no will to continue.

People in groups, who know the purpose for those groups, are able to maintain a sense of vision, a sense that the group is striving for a particular goal. Groups that lack this sense of vision may succeed in the short run, but over time they decline as different members begin to try to impose a purpose or goal on the group. The group may or may not buy into these purposes. If the group does not agree or if several people have different visions, then conflicts about why the group exists will inevitably arise. For this reason, statements of purpose are important for small groups as well as for churches and organizations. If people know why they are meeting together, they can choose to join that group and invest their time, their resources, and themselves in it. If the stated purpose is not what they wish to be a part of, then they do not need to be involved. But it is best to state such a purpose from the outset so that people understand it completely.

Recently I had a phone call from Donna. She complained about her small group saying that she wasn't getting deep Bible study in the meetings. She was very frustrated because the group leader scheduled time for socializing and talking to one another, for praying for one another, and for worshiping God together. But Donna wished for a very deep, intense Bible study. It would have been easy at that point to agree with her, saying, "Oh, I know that deep Bible study would be a good thing. I'll talk to that group leader tomorrow and have her adjust the program of the church to meet your needs." However, what Donna didn't understand was that Bible study was just *one* function of the group, albeit an important function. But the group existed for more than just Bible study.

One of the frustrations that I have had to contend with in the small group ministry is the perception that our small group program is a collection of Bible studies. This is flatly wrong in our context. It is not that we don't do Bible study within the small groups that function at Elmbrook Church. But people are very shortsighted if they think that Bible study is all we do within our program. Once Donna understood that the purpose for the small groups was much more than just Bible study, she was able to see not only the value of that group but also her own need for those other functions.

Importance to the Group
Provides Cohesion
Determining the purposes of the group provides a rallying point for the members of that group. If it is understood that one of the

SMALL GROUP DYNAMICS GRID

purposes for the existence of the small group is Bible study, then people understand that it is not only an important element, but they can invest themselves in this purpose. If it is not seen as extraneous, then group members will attend to what is being done and will not question the reason for doing Bible study. Having the purpose defined for the group allows the leader to call group members back to their purpose, thus bringing people back to the common understanding of their reason for being.

Secondly, an adequate definition of purpose provides motivation for the group. Some people are driven by forming solid relationships. If they can find a group where they can make friends and enjoy their company, then they will invest themselves in that kind of group. But some people aren't wired that way. They are driven by achieving goals and accomplishing purposes. Thus, for people bent in that direction, providing a clear set of purposes is motivating and prodding.

We must be careful to realize that neither personality type is wrong. Both are correct. It does matter how people are motivated and wired. It is a mistake to think that everyone should be a certain way as opposed to another. I tend to be wired in the direction of focusing on relationships. I have a good friend, Dave, who is tremendously organized and task oriented. Dave is a wonderful balance for me. We work so well together because I tone down any excesses related to accomplishing tasks, and he helps me get the job done! So we must recognize that for those people who have a need to know where they are going, we must give them that sense of direction.

Basis for Evaluation

Having a clearly defined statement of purpose for a group also provides a means for evaluation. Group leaders are able to evaluate where the group is at in relationship to a set of functions in which they are supposed to be engaging. They will find out whether or not they are accomplishing the goal that they have set out to reach. It cannot be overemphasized how important evaluation is.

The group that Donna was in regularly met to evaluate whether or not they were reaching the goals and purposes for which they gathered. The leaders, Bill and Vickie, were able to guide the members of that small group to an understanding of why they met. Then they were able to evaluate whether or not they were reaching the goal.

Evaluation can be done by leaders themselves, as Bill and Vickie did in evaluating their own perceptions of how well they were doing in reaching their goals. But it can also be done with a select group of people from a small group, a core group. The core group can meet to discuss whether or not they are reaching their goals. In fact, it is suggested that these people do meet in order to gain a reasonable vision of whether or not they are accomplishing what they have set out to do. A core group can consist of five to six people who gather on a quarterly or bimonthly basis to evaluate the overall health and state of the group. It is important that core group members be the ones committed to the group and who understand why the group is meeting. They also need to agree on the stated goals of the group. Then once there is agreement, they are able to evaluate whether or not they are reaching that goal.

Bill and Vickie, for example, regularly met with five or six people who were the key members of their group. Together they evaluated whether or not they maintained a reasonable balance of trying to attain each of the stated goals of the group.

This method is far preferable to the more common way of evaluating the group— asking all members to answer the question, "How do you feel the group is doing?" There are pitfalls of an open evaluation session for the whole group. Some people will not understand the reason the group exists and others will have a very skewed view of whether or not a group is achieving its stated goals. Their views can be excessively biased because of issues they are dealing with in their own lives, or perhaps they wish to change the focus of the group.

Marks of a Healthy Group

In a healthy group, the purpose is clear to all its members. It is obvious that the first step is making the purpose clear to the leadership of the small group network. That is, there must be an agreed upon set of goals and purposes that are adopted by all of the people who are to be involved in the leadership of these groups. Some groups may have different *emphases*, but overall direction should be clear in the minds of those who are forming the groups.

It is equally important that the set of purposes is specific. That is, a person will know when he has made significant strides toward accomplishing the purposes. It is not enough to just simply say this group exists to nurture one another, for instance. One person's definition of nurture may differ widely from another's. However, one could say that part of the function of this group is to provide fellowship through potluck suppers or through the sharing of prayer requests within the group. Or if the overall goal or purpose is to enhance fellowship within the group, then there must be a more specific statement of how that general purpose will be be reached. A specific, clear purpose must be achievable at a certain time. Thus, while a general goal may be to provide fellowship, a specific goal would be to exchange prayer requests on March 17.

People understand that the overall purposes of the small groups may be general. But there must be a specifying, if you will, a quantifying aspect to these purposes. Perhaps they can be called objectives, a narrowing down of how a group will reach the more general goals. In our situation, we have the goal of encouraging people to worship within their small groups. In order to make that specific, we must be clear that part of the meeting is going to provide opportunities for worship and adoration of God. So it is reasonable to state that the group will open any given meeting with prayers of praise or songs of adoration to the Lord. In so doing, they are accomplishing the overall purpose to provide a place for worship, but they are also able to accomplish, at least in part, the specific objective of providing a place of worship on a particular day through a particular method.

The purpose must also be stated in writing. When a group gets together it is extremely important that not just the leader understands what he or she is trying to do, but that the entire group also understands the goals. Consequently, it is appropriate to state the overall goals of the small group on a regular basis. As new people come into the group, they will understand the reason for its existence. They will understand, for instance, that whether they like singing or not is not the point. Rather, the point is whether or not the group provides a place of worship for people.

There is a corollary to the written statement of purpose. It must also be understood by the people within the group. That means there must be a clarification of the group's purposes and goals. And group members must offer feedback, indicating that these are understood and are worth investing in. Take the case of Donna, who was mentioned earlier and who desired deep Bible study. She was able to buy into the overall direction of the group because she also recognized her need for fellowship. She was able to invest herself in that group because she realized and understood the overall purpose for it.

Once group members understand the purpose, then it is more likely to become important to them. They will realize that what they are doing is extremely important and contributes to the overall health and well being of the group. In a recent leadership class which I led, one of the participants was Joe, who was already leading a group. Joe's group had some difficulties. The group had lost most of its members, and Joe became increasingly discouraged about where the group was going. But after discussing why people left his group, it began to flourish once again. The members understood why the group was meeting because this leader began to explain the reasons for the group's existence and what he would try to do to promote the overall life of the group. As a result, the membership was transformed. Joe ended up leading an almost new group since most of the other people had left. These newcomers were able to buy into Joe's group and invest themselves in it.

Joe brought Bob from their group to the leadership class. Bob commented after the class that he now finally realized what Joe was trying to accomplish. It was exciting to discover that Bob really wanted to do what Joe had been trying to do with his group. But one reason for the resistance from Joe's old group members was that they didn't understand why Joe was trying to do some of the things that he did.

The old members who had left did not understand what Joe was trying to do, especially when he expressed his frustration in anger toward them. But the group members are beginning to understand not only why they exist but also how they will accomplish their goals. They have a sense of unity as they all understand where they are going.

The last mark of a healthy group in relation to purpose is achievable goals. This mark is closely related to the idea that goals must be specific. For example, it is not reasonable to say that the group will, in the next three weeks, spend five 24-hour periods in prayer. Such a vision, while noble, will probably fail to gain the participation of the group members because it is not achievable.

Leaders can be either underachievers by not having enough to challenge their people or overachievers who set the goals so high that they discourage the group. In one of our small groups, the leader had decided to go through a particular book of the Bible verse by verse. This method could be frustrating to some if they think they will finish the entire book within a four-week period, or even within a year. This group took several years to accomplish what they set out to do. The goal they set was extremely high; it was achievable only as they took a long period of time to do it.

Guidelines for Leaders
The leader must first determine the purpose for his or her group. Most of the purposes for small groups within the church are set by the leadership of the church or by a group of leaders within the small group network. Enclosed at the end of this chapter is a set of guidelines which have been determined for the small group program at Elmbrook Church. It is not intended to be a model for other churches as much as it is intended to describe the overall ministry of the small groups that exist at the church. Hopefully they give insight into how to construct a set of goals and objectives for other small group programs.

Once the purpose has been determined and the group leader has decided to follow it, then the next step is to communicate that purpose to the group. As was mentioned before, regular meetings describing what the group is trying to do may be very helpful at this point. It is also beneficial to have the person coordinating all of the small groups to attend periodically and discuss why the leadership has determined the stated purposes. I believe the purposes need to be established by leadership of a local church that is doing small group ministry and that such decisions not be left to an individual group. If the church has a workable small group philosophy and definite goals, then the leadership can communicate these effectively to the groups. With such specific direction and oversight, there is a far greater chance of the groups actually accomplishing their purposes.

Finally, regular evaluation times not only serve to provide mid-course corrections for the group, but they also accomplish the communication of the purposes to the group. A good leader will suggest a time of evaluation, but he will provide the guidelines by which the group is to be evaluated. In this way, group members can discuss the question, "What are we supposed to be doing, and are we accomplishing it? Also, those who may not understand why the group exists are able to discuss its purpose for themselves.

Times of evaluation also provide the impetus for group leaders to keep moving toward the overall purpose and stated goals of the small group. The group that understands their reason for being understands the goals for which they are aiming. The group that understands their goals is able to evaluate whether or not they are reaching these goals. These groups will be able to move in the direction of accomplishing what they have set out to do. The adage, "If you aim at nothing, you will most certainly achieve it," is true also in small group ministries. So let's be determined in what we are trying to do and in pushing our groups toward achieving those goals.

The following section states the goal and objectives of the small group program at Elmbrook Church. It is intended to give a taste of how to develop and define purposes for groups. Reference is made to the Neighborhood Groups (abbreviated NHGs) which make up one aspect of the small group ministry. The other small groups — the couples' groups, singles' groups, and college and career age groups — all follow similar guidelines.

The Functions of a Neighborhood Group

FUNCTION #1: A shared commitment to God's PEOPLE
EVIDENCES: Sharing with and caring for one another, often called fellowship
BIBLICAL BASIS: (1) *Jesus' command* that we love one another as He loved us and so demonstrate that we are His disciples (John 13:34-35)
(2) *Jesus' prayer* that we as His disciples

might become one with each other just as the Trinity is one (John 17:20-23)

EXPRESSIONS: (not exhaustive):
— Hospitality (use of home, greeting one another, preparing/serving)
— Potluck dinners, refreshments
— Prayer (sharing one's needs with others in the group, praying for others' needs)
— Sharing (verbally expressing what God has been doing in your lives recently, tangibly sharing physical resources with others)
— Weekend retreats
— Bearing one another's burdens
— Speaking the truth in love
— Accepting one another (their differences and likes)
— Forgiving one another

FUNCTION #2: A shared commitment to God's PURPOSES

EVIDENCES: Discovering and applying God's Word to accomplish His will for His Church; often called instruction

BIBLICAL BASIS: (1) One of God's purposes is that we might become like Him so that we might glorify Him. To enable us to be what He wants us *to be,* He gives us the fruit of the Spirit (Galatians 5:22-23).
(2) God has also purposed that we might *do* good works in order to build up His people and to expand His kingdom. To enable us *to do* what He wants us to, He gives each believer a gift of the Spirit (1 Peter 4:10).

EXPRESSIONS: (not exhaustive)
— Love, joy, peace, patience, kindness, goodness, faithfulness, gentleness, and self-control (evidenced by the believer at group meetings and during the week)

      — Discovery of spiritual gifts (helping one another to recognize your gifts)

      — Development of spiritual gifts (taking or making opportunities to develop your spiritual gifts through trial and error, teaching, working with others, etc.)

      — Deployment of spiritual gifts (taking or making opportunities to use your gifts for the upbuilding of the body of Christ as directed by Christ the Head)

      — Bible study with an emphasis on application of God's Word (becoming a "doer of the Word," sharing insights with others in the group, listening to others' insights)

FUNCTION #3: A shared commitment to God's PERSON

EVIDENCES: Worshiping God and giving to Him that of which He is worthy, often called consecration

BIBLICAL BASIS: (1) Jesus said that the Father is seeking true worshipers who worship Him in spirit and truth, that is, those who worship Him through both their *attitudes* and their *actions* (John 4:23-24).

(2) We are reminded that it is our reasonable worship to present to God as a sacrifice our bodies and our minds in order to know and do His will (Romans 12:1-2).

EXPRESSIONS: (not exhaustive)

      — Testimonies (giving praise for who God is as well as for what He has done)

      — Singing (psalms, hymns, and spiritual songs)

      — Communion (remembering Christ's work on the cross for us)

      — Repentance (admitting your sins)

      — Confession (public, as appropriate, and turning your back on known sin)

      — Praise/adoration

— Intercession

— Sacrifice (laying on God's altar all your possessions for His use, including time, money, home, car, etc.)

— Offerings (giving your resources to men, as well as to God as He supplies)

FUNCTION #4: A shared commitment to God's PROGRAM

EVIDENCES: Serving one another in God's family and reaching out to the unreached; often called Christian service

BIBLICAL BASIS: (1) Inreach: Reaching in to help and serve hurting members of God's family is His priority. Galatians 6:10 says, "As we have opportunity, let us do good to all people, especially to those who belong to the family of believers." (2) Outreach: Reaching out to those not yet in God's family, while reaching up to Him as an extension of His grace, is also important (Matthew 28:18-20; Acts 1:8).

EXPRESSION: (not exhaustive)

— Personal evangelism (at home, at school, on the job, in the neighborhood, etc.)

— Corresponding with and caring for your group's missionaries

— Hospital visitation

— Nursing home/prison ministries

— Rescue mission work

— Resettling refugees (Matthew 25:31-46)

— Caring for widows

The Neighborhood Group

I. NHGs defined

A. What they are not

1. A substitute for a midweek service

2. A home Bible study

3. A social gathering

4. A rescue mission to reach one's neighborhood

5. A group for SOS needs
6. A counseling agency
7. A group therapy session
8. An interest group

(While all of the above functions are valid activities of NHGs, no single function can effectively define the purpose of a NHG.)

B. What they are

1. A building (Ephesians 2:19-22)

The *structural* aspect of a NHG is a building; Christ's relationship to the group is that of the cornerstone. He is the One around whom the group is built. Whatever the structure or form a NHG takes, it must always be centered around the chief cornerstone.

2. A bride (Ephesians 5:22-32)

The *relational* aspect of a NHG is similar to that of a bride and bridegroom. We are called the bride, and Christ is the Bridegroom. This relationship implies at least two things: commitment and provision. Provisions stem from commitment, and commitment comes from relationship. Of course, the relationship and the commitment that follows is designed to be mutual. It begins as we accept His provisions for us.

3. A body (Ephesians 5:23, 30; 1:22-23)

The *functional* aspect of a NHG is a body composed of several members with Christ as the Head. In Ephesians 4, two facts stand out about the functioning of the body, particularly the body of Christ: its unity and its diversity. Unity exists in the midst of diversity and is supplied by the Spirit of God. The *fruit* of the Spirit is designed to make us all alike (like God) and the *gifts* of the Spirit are designed to make us all different!

Vital Signs of Life in a Growing Neighborhood Group

Check those items which apply to the group you evaluate.

Purpose One: A Shared Commitment to God's People (sharing and caring)

_____ Conversation included testimonies to God's faithfulness.

_____ Individuals shared personal concerns with the group.

_____ People shared how insights gained from Scripture affected their personal lives.

_____ People were relaxed about sharing and showed interest in each other.

_____ Members showed evidence of living out biblical "one another" commands.

_____ Visitors were adequately introduced and welcomed.

_____ An atmosphere of warmth prevailed and members seemed to enjoy one another's friendship.

_____ When people expressed needs, members responded appropriately to them.

_____ Participants seemed to have contact with each other during the week.

_____ People prayed for one another's needs.

_____ Other: _____

Purpose Two: A Shared Commitment to God's Purposes (discovering and applying)

_____ Insights into Scripture were related to current, real-life situations, not just adding to head knowledge.

_____ Evidence of the fruit of the Spirit was seen in the way the group related to each other. Circle the characteristics you specifically observed: love, joy, peace, patience, kindness, goodness, faithfulness, gentleness, self-control.

_____ The Bible study led members to discover truths for themselves.

_____ The Bible discussion proceeded by contributions in response to the text and one another, rather than solely to and through the leader.

_____ Spiritual gifts were in operation. What gifts did you observe and how many people were involved in the exercise of the gifts other than the leader? _____

_____

_____

_____ Other: _____

Purpose Three: A Shared Commitment to God's Person (worshiping and giving)

A. Attitudes (in Spirit)

_____ Spirit of thanksgiving and gratitude

_____ Spirit of praise in testimonies and prayer

_____ Spirit of confession/humility/forsaking of sin

_____ Spirit of intercession; circle the ones you witnessed: missionaries, group member, church, themselves

_____ Spirit of singing with enthusiasm and understanding

_____ Spirit of submission to Christ's lordship (He's in control; acknowledgment of such)

_____ Spirit of expectancy of answered prayer (faith/dependence)

_____ Spirit of Christ-centered conversation throughout the evening.

B. Activities (in truth/deed)

_____ Psalms, hymns, and spiritual songs were read, sung, or used in the evening's worship.

_____ Prayer was actually a vital part of the group life.

_____ Communion was celebrated by the group.

_____ People offered their services in response to needs (practical worship) by:

____ Opening their home ____ Visiting the sick

____ Giving their time ____ Caring for widows, etc.

____ Using their gifts ____ Other: _____

____ Preparing meals _____

Purpose Four: A Shared Commitment to God's Program (serving and reaching)

A. Evidences of inreach (to group members and other members of the family of believers)

_____ Action taken to meet needs expressed by group members ("legs to prayers"), i.e., meals, transportation, baby-sitting

———— Hospital visitation planned (when appropriate)
———— Contact with missionaries
    ———— Prayer for, interest in, concern for
    ———— Reading (or paraphrasing) of their letters, needs, etc.
———— Correspondence *to* as well as *from* evident
———— Projects to meet special needs (e.g., baby showers) or for special occasions (e.g., holidays, birthdays)
———— Involvement as a group with projects in the church at large
———— Follow-up of new members or new converts
———— Other ———————————————————

B. Evidences of outreach (to those outside the family of God)
———— Evangelistic Bible studies
———— Nursing home services
———— Prison ministries (writing/visiting)
———— Resettling refugees
———— Food, clothes, furniture for the poor
———— Ministries of social justice (political concerns with social implications, e.g., issues on abortion, euthanasia)
———— Sharing faith in Christ at school, home, work, etc.
———— Other: ———————————————————

After evaluating this group, the thing I am most thankful to God for is:

————————————————————————————

————————————————————————————

The main thing that needs prayer and work (from my perspective) is:

————————————————————————————

————————————————————————————

Review and Reflection
    1. What are the purposes for your small group(s)? Are these written out and understood by the people within your group?

2. What can happen if a purpose is well understood by the leader of a group but not understood at all by the group members?
3. How can we handle those who disagree with the stated purposes for the small group? How should we feel if a person leaves the group over such a conflict in philosophy?
4. In what ways can a core group of people be helpful to keep a group on the right track? In what ways can this core group be a source of safety and security for the leader?
5. In evaluating your group, have the stated goals and purposes been achieved? If not, how can the group attain such goals? Are they realistic? What can be done to more effectively communicate these goals and purposes to the group?
6. In the light of the proposed set of goals at the end of this chapter, are your goals right for you in your situation? What is on target? What needs changing?

FIVE

COMMUNICATION FOR EDIFICATION

Let us therefore make every effort to do what leads to peace and to mutual edification (Romans 14:19).

Many pastors really love to dream. They dream about what their church will be like five years from now. They dream about changes that can be made in worship services. They dream about changes of personnel in certain areas. Most pastors also dream about trying different approaches to ministry. Or at times they visualize moving into different areas of ministry. These dreams remain dreams, however. The problem is not so much a shortage of ideas in the church as it is a shortage of resources—human resources.

The true visionaries of the church, both on the professional level (pastors) and on the lay level, are vital to the church. However, visionary types must link with the practical doers in the congregation. But doers generally are not automatically attracted to visionaries. Doers tend to be cautious, methodical, and careful. Visionary types are bold, risky, adventuresome. Mixing the two is a key to

SMALL GROUP DYNAMICS GRID

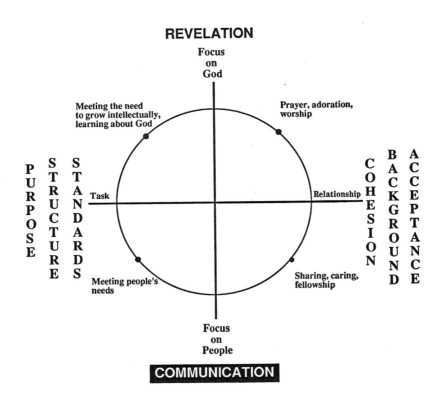

accomplishing effective ministry, whether it is church leadership and the congregation or small group leaders and their little flocks.

This is not to say that small group leaders are always visionary types. They are not. However, a well functioning small group will have tasks to accomplish, whether they have been set by bold visionary types or by doers. It is the responsibility of the small group leader to link the resources that exist within that group with the tasks that need to be accomplished. The key to forming that link is communication.

Levels of Communication

In order to promote effective communication, a group leader needs to understand the various levels of disclosure. The least threatening level is sharing of ideas. For instance, a person might say, "I think patience is the most important virtue." Although others may disagree, this statement is not nearly as threatening as the second level, the sharing of personal experiences. At this level, we open ourselves up to the group in a very vulnerable way. The next level involves sharing current problems and feelings not related to the group or someone in it.

The fourth level of communication is sharing feelings toward group members. This situation can be very uncomfortable for both the leader and group members. But, handled in an appropriate way, groups can operate at this level. Finally, the deepest level is the sharing of very personal problems not ordinarily discussed outside of the family.

Importance of Communication for the Group

If you made a list of some of the least effective ways of finding the resources that exist in a congregation, the one at the top has to be the church bulletin announcement. The word gets out, but usually the request is for volunteers. Although most small groups do not have a written bulletin, they do schedule times for announcements. If you attend enough small groups, you will note that announcements proliferate. It is as if the Sunday morning model of including lengthy announcements has been transferred to the small group living room.

Verbal announcements are not quite as ineffective as written ones, but they still are largely without power. Thus, while there may be many appeals to meet a need or accomplish a task, they largely go unheeded because the method of communication is poor.

One leader, for example, complained that for weeks he had been appealing for help in a certain area; but it never came. After that, discouragement set in. He focused on the lack of assistance being offered by his group. However, the problem was not that people were unwilling to help, but they were not being drawn into the task through the proper means of communicating. Had the communication pattern been personal, specific, and meaningful, the results would have been much better.

In this particular group, the leader was so frustrated that he became bitter. People decided to leave the group rather than be targets of criticism when they walked through the door on Friday evenings. If the need had been handled properly, the leader would have been able to gain the assistance that he desperately needed; and the group would have been unified. However, with poor communication, unwanted static dominated the scene.

For Developing Unity
John was part of a group that had the responsibility of preparing young engaged couples for marriage. The task was a monumental one since most of the young couples had the attitude that they did not need any help in preparing for a lifetime commitment together. Most felt that they were going along just fine, thank you; and any suggestion that they might possibly have problems down the line was totally absurd.

Working with such couples could at times be discouraging if it were not for a small group who banded together to talk about these starry eyed men and women and the issues they would face. Bill, being one of the newcomers to this group, found it extremely refreshing when he was able to talk to other leaders about the problems and issues that had surfaced in his dealings with these engaged couples. A tremendous amount of camaraderie developed quickly within that group because they shared a common task.

Bill and his wife, Susie, beamed at the opportunity to minister to these couples. One of the reasons for their extreme enthusiasm was the input from other leaders in this small group. They saw the vitality that others who were trying to work with these engaged couples had, and the enthusiasm was downright contagious.

What was communicated to Bill and Susie was that this was an important ministry. It was a ministry that required bonding between the leaders and demanded a positive attitude toward the couples with whom they were dealing. Were these elements discussed with Bill and Susie as they launched into this area of ministry? Yes, of course. However, far more was communicated by others who shared the vision, talked about the joys of working with engaged couples, and talked about the enrichment to their own lives. The excitement of the people who were already involved carried over to Bill and Susie. There was tremendous unity among those leaders.

Soon after they became involved with the group Bill developed cancer. One Friday night shortly before his surgery, the entire group of leaders gathered to discuss the plight of some of the engaged couples they would be dealing with when another premarital class began. But it wasn't all business that evening. These leaders banded together in unity and with tender care. The group gathered around Bill to encourage him, to pray for him, to cry with him, to simply touch him.

The backgrounds of these leaders were very different. But effective communication helped build unity within the group. Such unity had developed that Bill felt free to share what he was going through—the fear and joy that he experienced and the confidence he had in the Lord Jesus. As a result, the group ministered to him in a deep way. Four days after major cancer surgery, Bill was back ministering to those engaged couples and receiving encouragement and strength from his group of leaders.

In John 17, the Lord Jesus appealed for unity among His disciples. Such an appeal communicated its importance. Unity is expressed in many ways and, in part, is related to the area of acceptance discussed previously. One communicates unity through showing acceptance of one another.

But unity can also exist when there are differences of opinion within a small group. It is the way that diversity of opinion is expressed that affects the overall unity. Communicating effectively on even widely differing opinions on nonessential issues need not diminish a sense of unity.

A number of years ago, I was a member of a church but not on the staff. When I went to my first congregational meeting, I was shocked to discover the members were dividing over an issue of "obvious importance": Should the women host baby showers for one another? People were strongly divided on this issue. Although it was not in the church constitution, it seemed to carry the same importance as an article of doctrine. We laugh about the absurdity of such an issue. However, many small groups divide themselves over equally foolish ones. Leaders need to be aware of how to control communication without hindering it and to be able to discern major issues from minor ones.

Handling Problems

Ignore it, and it will go away. That's one philosophy for handling problems within small groups. The only problem is that you can't and it will not. Difficulties experienced in a small group are like physical maladies. Some are sores that need to be treated gently; others are more serious and need direct, aggressive procedures. And the most extreme forms of problems within small groups may need drastic measures. If there is a good communication base, these measures, be they extreme or minor, carry a great deal of effectiveness. Even the most difficult problems can be lessened in their impact through proper channels of communication.

Michelle happened to be one of those moderate problems within a small group. She tended to be moody, opinionated, easily hurt, and frustrated. And if that weren't enough, she was vocal. One good thing you could say about her is that, as a leader, you always knew where you stood from Michelle's perspective. She always let you know her opinion.

Yet her very verbal nature was causing severe problems within the group. People were having difficulty dealing with that type of behavior. However, with good, clear instructions on the procedures to follow in order to curb Michelle's freely given opinions, the group was able to continue. And Michelle did not feel slighted.

The adage, "If you ask for criticism, you will get it," is certainly true at this point. It is important to schedule times for feedback within a small group in order to find out just how the group is doing. However, it is not helpful if the impression is given that such criticism and opinions are solicited at any time. There are times when a group should acquiesce and follow the suggested approach developed by the group. And there are times when leaders are simply to be followed even though there may be some dissent.

If someone like Michelle should want to continually give advice or, as she would put it, "constructive criticism," affirmation can be given: Yes, we are interested in suggestions; but no, not at this time. The suitable form or tool of communication can be given to her at a more appropriate time. In this way, Michelle is affirmed that her opinion is desired. However, such opinions need to yield to the group task or function at that particular moment. Michelle, in being dealt with gently over a period of two years, has toned down. She has realized that she doesn't always need to give her opinion.

The patterns of communication gain a highlighted sense of importance when such problems exist. Thus, whether a group is informing a critical person that time for evaluation will be made available or reminding a very talkative person that a time for sharing prayer concerns is for all to have a chance to speak, it thereby is recognizing the importance of communication for handling difficulties.

Marks of a Healthy Group
There are several marks of a healthy group in relation to communication patterns. First of all, group communication must be total. As an adjunct faculty member of a seminary, I have the opportunity to teach in a graduate school or college level educational setting. It is remarkable that you can walk into such a setting and the "rules" seem to permeate the atmosphere.

Students all sit in rows; they generally do not talk too much with each other. They have a tendency to read a lot at their tables or chairs. They listen attentively, and remarkably they all seem to raise their hands when they have something to say. This is quite strange when you think of it because in most conversations we don't raise our hands before we speak.

When we wish to talk in a small group, we don't sit in an aloof fashion, pretending not to notice the other people and only talk to the leader as a student may talk to a teacher. In most conversations, the whole group carries a great deal of importance. Therefore, people must address the whole group.

In the university setting, the instructor carries all the authority. When confronted with opportunities to lead a small group, many people object, saying "I could never teach a small group." What they really are saying is that they would not be able to perform the educational role with which they are familiar. In most classes, the instructor imparts knowledge; the students sit and absorb. Occasionally there is feedback, but it is given directly to the instructor; and the instructor responds back to the individual. The communication pattern in such a situation is clearcut, at many times inviolable, and fosters a limited view of how education is accomplished.

Not so with the small group. The aim for a healthy group is to provide total, open communication. It is not good for communication to be one way, that is, from the leader to the participants. Nor should we simply strive for communication between the leader and one or two group members. The mark of a healthy group is communication occurring between all parties and not always in response to the leader's suggestions but spontaneously as well.

Total communication refers to all areas of group life. That is, everyone participates in the sharing and caring and worship. Each person finds freedom to share personal needs and questions regarding the Scriptures. Total communication enables the group to foster a tremendous amount of acceptance between each other.

Communication must not only be total but also open. Open refers to the fact that members do not feel hindered by any others within the group. This situation does not mean that we don't at times restrict the communication patterns. But for the most part, people are free to express themselves whenever they want to.

The group's communication must also be done in a loving manner. Scripture says that speaking the truth in love is of paramount importance. If communication that is total and open is linked with a loving attitude among small group members, the net effect is the building up of one another in truth and a bolstering of self-esteem.

Guidelines for Leaders
Modeling by the Leader
When it comes to insuring good communication patterns in a group, we can rely on much advice that is simply common sense. However,

as one person said, "Common sense is not so common anymore." The first point for the small group leader is to make sure that he or she is modeling good communication. That is, the leader herself decides that if her group is going to become all that it should be before the Lord, then she must have open communication with group members. In so doing, she is—with God's help—loving that group, a fact that is obvious through her verbal and nonverbal communication. Failure to do so contributes to the death of a group.

William, for example, experienced a failure. This failure was due in part to the inability to open up and explain his frustrations regarding the group, the direction of the group, and the response of the group. William had difficulty being open; he had difficulty in loving that group. And it came out in the way he led them.

For William, it was of supreme importance to make sure that all the duties of the evening were cared for. However, what he communicated to the group members was that duty was far more important than the relationships that were being established. This attitude came out in the way he modeled communication. The modeling that he did was not helpful to the group, and the group in time resented the way that he communicated with them. In the end, the group rebelled against him, disbanded, and reformed later under new leadership.

Such a failure is always painful but it highlights the difficulty the leader had in modeling good communication. Because he was not open with the group and was not openly caring and providing total communication, the group itself was not honest with William.

Marvin, on the other hand, acted quite differently. He regularly communicated what the group was to accomplish, why they did certain things, and the importance of the caring aspect of a small group. He emphasized that care is shown through good communication. The results within the group are striking. Group members are open with one another and care for one another. They have in many ways taken on the personality of the leader.

When we look at the Lord Jesus we see similar modeling. In his discussions with the Samaritan woman at the well in John 4, Jesus modeled both an open way of communicating with her as well as a very loving, true, and caring attitude. He broke the rule of His day that said Jewish people don't associate with Samaritans or prostitutes. Not only did he associate with her, but He did so in loving concern.

His communication of truth with the woman at the well was incisive but not offensive. She responded positively to His modeling by telling others about the message of this man Jesus. She went to her village and said, "Come, see a man who told me everything I ever did" (John 4:29). She was shocked at what He communicated to her.

But the message was packaged in such a way that she could hear it. Jesus was a model of combining difficult words with loving care. A small group leader should follow His example. As a result, others will begin to pick up on how the leader expresses himself or herself and speak and act in like manner.

Standards for Communication

But modeling itself may not be enough since it can be missed by certain people. While it is extremely important for a small group leader to model good communication, some people within the group will take it for granted and simply go on with their own patterns. They do not recognize that they may be hindering total, open, loving communication within the group. For such people—and we all fit into this category at some time or another—we need to establish standards that should be followed within the group for maximizing good communication.

Most small groups are composed of people from a variety of backgrounds. Consequently, in order to most effectively deal with people from diverse backgrounds, it is not inappropriate to establish a procedure for speaking about one's background within the group.

It is most often necessary when there is a discussion that may reveal differences in theology or interpretation of biblical texts due to to people's religious backgrounds. This fact became particularly evident in focus in one group where there were people from "Brand X" denomination. The leader unwittingly began to criticize this particular group, saying that people in it have certain obvious theological problems. Now it was inappropriate at that point to so bluntly and insensitively speak about another's background.

These comments caused much agitation, and the pastor in

charge of group ministries heard about the inappropriate comments. The result was a breakdown in communication. The leader did not provide an atmosphere of total love and communication. Instead, he squelched those people from Brand X denomination who had so much to offer to the group.

It is no wonder that they were put on the defensive, and it is only natural for them to be reluctant to participate totally in the group. Such a problem could be averted with a simple rule established when a group is formed. For example, we will not talk about denominational backgrounds. But if we refer to a religious group, simply call it "Brand X" denomination.

The focus ought not to be on the problems with any one church or background but rather on the positive aspects of its teaching. This point is particularly true in reference to public testimonies within small groups. A leader should work with individuals who are going to give a testimony as to how they came to faith in Christ. In dealing with them lovingly, wording can be changed so as not to offend those who may truly value the particular background that the testifiers disdain. Such caution and evaluation of what will be said is vital for the overall ministry of a small group.

Another issue that might come up in a group is whether or not to raise hands before speaking. For example, I ministered in a small group within a church that had a fairly formal structure and participation patterns in worship. I was struck by the fact that before they said anything, the members all raised their hands.

Because of their backgrounds, they always raised their hands before asking or answering a question or commenting in any Bible class. This response was not wrong, although it was uncomfortable for me since I was not from that background. So quickly I set a standard for communication by saying, "You don't need to raise your hands in this group. I know that some wish to do so, and that is fine. But you don't need to." The standard I requested was for unhindered communication, shared when they wished.

Another situation that requires a standard is when group members are intent on cutting off others before they are done speaking. The leader must make it clear that it is important to hear everyone who wishes to speak and it is not courteous to cut off one another. More standards for communication are in chapter 9.

Handling Conflict

Conflict is often feared in groups; people are very uncomfortable when it occurs. However, it is necessary to remember that conflict is *not* a sign of unspirituality or immaturity. Conflict does *not* signal the group's demise or indicate that there is weak leadership. Conflict is inevitable and an indication that there are differences in thinking, goals, opinions, ideas, needs, etc. It is an opportunity for the group to mature. It can help group members grow in commitment to one another, in love, in communication, and in interpersonal relationships. Working through conflict involves giving people the opportunity to be heard. Leaders must evaluate why conflicts exist, brainstorm with others about possible solutions, evaluate the offered solutions, and then implement them.

David Augsburger, in his book *Caring Enough to Confront* (Regal Books, 1981), says that there are five typical ways of dealing with conflict between people. These patterns vary according to the importance of meeting goals (the reason for the conflict) and keeping relationships. These five ways are summarized below:

1. "I'll get him." This I win/you lose approach assumes that in every conflict, one side is totally right and the other is totally wrong. The ones who think they are right feel obliged to set the others straight. The result is that some meet their goals while others lose theirs.

2. "I'll get out." This approach views conflict as basically hopeless: People do not change. Therefore, conflicts are to be avoided at all costs. So when they occur, one needs to overlook the difficulty or withdraw from the situation. The result is that one side meets its goal but loses the relationship, and the other side loses both the goal and the relationship.

3. "I'll give in." This approach views conflicts as disastrous to relationships. Because it puts such a high priority on relationships, it typically gives in to the other person's opinions and desires. Its goal is to "be nice." The result is that one party meets its goal, and the other party misses out.

4. "I'll meet you halfway." This approach tries to accomplish a creative compromise when there is conflict. It assumes that neither party has the whole truth on the issue. It attempts to preserve the

relationship and obtain the goals. It results in both sides winning something and both sides losing something.

5. "I care enough to confront." This approach places a high priority on both relationship and integrity. Conflict is viewed as being neutral—neither good nor bad. It attempts to work through the differences with the assumption that what both sides perceive and want are important. It results in both sides winning because goals are met and the relationship is strengthened (Regal Books, 1981, pp. 13–15).

If group leaders can keep these suggestions in view, then conflict will be handled more easily. There is a tension between task and relationships. There are times when relationships are broken because of the importance of the task. But often both the needs of relationships and the need to accomplish a task can be maintained.

Leading Discussions

Effective discussions do not just happen. Rather, they are guided by leaders who understand a few basic tips. First, he or she makes sure that each member of the group is understood before another one speaks. It is too easy to let someone speak and not acknowledge, comment, or affirm what that person has said before moving on to another person's comment. Sometimes conversations do jump around with little acknowledgment that we have heard one another. This situation is not good for a small group.

In order to gain the most effective communication possible, leaders must be sure that others have indeed been heard. This is not too difficult to do in a small group. The leader just needs to be attuned to the overall atmosphere, asking the question, "Are people really being attentive to what others are saying, or are they simply waiting for their turn to speak?"

Another question a leader should ask himself is, "Are there a lot of discussions going on outside the main one?" That is, have little conversations broken out around the room? If so, the leader can simply say, "Now listen folks, are we sure we are hearing what Mary has to say? I know that what she is expressing here is important for our conversation." Unfortunately, it is too easy to go on to another's comments without really acknowledging those comments made by the last speaker.

Leaders can also seek to promote total communication through simple exercises like paraphrasing or repeating another person's comments. If something is mentioned only once, the group may miss it. However, if we rephrase that comment, particularly if it is a good one, we can both affirm the value of that communication as well as drive home the importance of listening. Another way of insuring total communication is to ask people to repeat what they have said if there is the feeling that others were not paying attention.

Another strategy for promoting discussion is to break larger groups into smaller ones. Even a group of ten people can be split into smaller groups to foster a greater openness and more involvement. One way to do this is through neighbor nudging. To use this method, ask everyone to discuss a question with the person sitting next to him. People are not as intimidated talking to one person as they are to the whole group, even if it's only a group of 10.

Almost every group has at least one "little no peep" who does not participate in discussions. The question of how to encourage such people to speak is asked often in small group leadership training seminars. The most common answer is to call on these people, thinking this action will draw them out. Usually the ones who make this suggestion have no problem sharing their own thoughts within a small group. But while this action may succeed in getting a person who never says anything to talk, it may actually hinder total, open, loving communication. The silent person may have a good reason for not speaking.

To call on someone is an intrusion into his life. Even to ask someone to read a section of Scripture aloud is taboo. A leader usually does not know, especially in the case of newcomers, whether or not a person is a good reader or can read at all. It is far better to ask for volunteers and to wait for the silent person to share of his own accord than to assume that our timetable for that person to speak is the correct one. We may, however, want to ask the quiet person to read a Scripture passage or prepare to pray at a future meeting. Thus we give him or her a chance to personally say yes or no to a request for involvement.

In contrast there is the dominating group member. An overbearing person can completely stifle a group and therefore must be controlled. Although it is not difficult to do so, the procedure may be threatening for a leader.

For example, Julie was the leader of a small group of couples and singles in their 50s and 60s. She came to me to ask how to handle Mary who felt that she had to answer every question and read every Scripture passage. Whenever there seemed to be a possible error in interpretation, she was the one who corrected it. And if someone tended not to be spiritual enough in the way he approached his own problems, she would call him on it. As a result, the group began to dwindle in numbers. When asked why they were leaving, group members said it was because of Mary's actions.

It was not difficult to discern that the group's survival depended on how we handled Mary and her problem of always having to be the one with the answer, the correct interpretation, or the right approach. We cannot assume a person like Mary is aware of this tendency. However, she may have other motives that we need to consider. She may sense that the group is going off the deep end in certain interpretations or that the leader is handling something improperly.

Though it was a difficult action to take, Julie needed to discuss these issues with Mary personally. She needed to confront Mary in a loving fashion, saying something like this: "I am trying to get maximum participation within this group. Because you are answering questions so much of the time or correcting what in your mind may be faulty interpretations, the group communication is being stifled. I need you to be quiet at times in order to solicit more responses from others. This will help us to draw the group out to be the caring and sharing kind of group that it needs to be." These are hard words, but need to be said at times.

Most people aren't as extreme in the way they approach their group involvement as Mary was. There are times when people simply need to be curbed in the way they interact with the group. If someone is dominating conversations, the leader may ask, "Does someone else have something to add?" Or he may approach this person outside the group setting and say, "Mark, I know that you have a lot of good things to say. However, we really are trying to get other people to share what they think. Can I enlist your help in drawing others out?" The personal, caring, loving approach outside of the group meeting can be the best way of handling the domineering person.

Building Relationships

Another tool for building total, open, loving communication is to plan times for informal interaction and fun in order to build relationships and gain one another's trust and acceptance. This may be as easy as using opener questions. These are used to get people to talk about some area of their lives that could be of interest to others in the group. Such opener questions can be answered by anyone; there are no right or wrong answers. They demand varying degrees of openness, depending on the stage of the group, and foster a sense of acceptance among the members.

For instance, the leader may ask a question like this at the beginning of a group meeting: "What is your name and what did you do at 2:00 this afternoon?" Such a question accomplishes a couple of communication goals. First, we recognize a person as he or she shares answers. Also, we begin to make links with people who are somewhat like us and begin to see the value of those who might be very unlike us. Whether someone is spending time observing the quality of machinery coming across an assembly line in a factory at 2:00 or putting the kids down for a nap, we begin to get a glimpse into his or her life. As a result, we can begin to understand where that person is coming from.

Such opener questions must be thought out very carefully, yet they are not difficult to devise. For instance, the question, "What did you do at 2:00 this afternoon?" is far better than asking the question, "What do you do for a living?" The latter one causes people to place value on an individual according to his profession or vocation. But a question like the first one does not lead to such a value judgment.

Certainly we should be above such value judgments, but they do occur even within the church. A person who sits in a small group where people are answering the question, "What do you do for a living?" may be extremely intimidated. For instance, if people are responding, "I am the vice-president of First National Bank," or "I am a physician and spend long hours at the hospital," others may answer, "Well, I'm just a _____." Those who, in the eyes of the world, do not have such prestigious jobs, may feel intimidated by those who seemingly have great power and wealth. The church must be a place where we move beyond such worldly distinctions. The construction of questions to help us understand who we are in Christ and not in the eyes of the world is crucial.

One of the joys of my ministry is to meet with leaders on an informal basis to learn more about them. Doing so enables me to have better communication with them when it is time to discuss issues related to group leadership. It is always a delight to go out and enjoy a meal with people in order to find out what they are like and what their dreams and desires are. Such investment of time, whether it be from pastor to group leader or group leader to group member, pays off in the long run, especially if difficulties arise with that person.

When unpleasant or critical information needs to be communicated to people or groups, it will be received more readily if trust and acceptance have been built up through such informal times. Consequently, we leaders should plan social activities for the entire group as well. People naturally begin to talk and communicate with each other and care for each other in such unstructured times.

For example, one of the small groups at my church invited me to a Milwaukee Brewers baseball game. I was delighted to see these people in a nonchurch or non-small group setting. We sat in the stands and talked about a host of different issues, from the horrible plight of the Brewers to the concerns people had about their parents to problems they had in dealing with a child.

Fortunately, the idea that the only time that matters is quality time is beginning to wane. People are recognizing more and more that quantity time spent with individuals is as important as the quality of that time. Getting people together in a non group atmosphere also enables us to show acceptance of them at all points in their lives. We are able to show that we care for them even if it is not the scheduled meeting time.

Evaluating the Group
Another helpful guideline for the leader is to intentionally endeavor to talk about group problems, successes, and tasks occasionally with the group in order to discover what members think about such

items. A group leader may say, "I really think we have not made enough efforts in the area of evangelism." But the group's perception may be that the leader is always pushing them in that direction. If he or she continues to push, there will be resentment. Instead, the topic may be discussed during a group meeting by saying, "What do you think about my ideas for promoting greater evangelism by this group?" The group then is able to respond in an open, loving, caring fashion by replying, "We already have that kind of emphasis, and we need to keep from losing sight of other emphases within our group."

The point is not how much evangelism a group should sponsor but talking about this kind of issue as a group in order to promote communication. A leader could adopt the guideline of spending 10 minutes every 4 or 5 meetings to ask questions such as the following:

- How well are we on track?
- Have we accomplished what we set out to do?
- If not, in what area are we lacking?
- How would you feel if you were a newcomer in this group? (if the group is seeking new people)
- Do you feel that we provide opportunities for everyone to express themselves? Why or why not?
- Do you feel accepted in this group? Why or why not?
- What problems do we need to talk about?

By asking these simple questions, communication lines can be kept open. Also, those that are clogged can be rooted out and freed from whatever hindrance might be binding the group.

Review and Reflection
1. As you review the communication patterns in the group(s) in which you participate, what needs to be affirmed and changed?
2. What procedures for communication are understood within the group? Are there some that need to be stated in light of this chapter?
3. How does your group handle conflict? Are there those who need to be confronted about their communication patterns?

4. How are you handling those who are reluctant to become involved in group discussions? How are you handling dominant people?
5. Would the people in your group say that they are free to contribute in the meetings? What can you do to help others open up to the group?
6. Is your group providing times for informal interaction? What can you do to maximize communication in the group?

Six

DEVELOPING STRUCTURES TO FACILITATE GROUPS

Instead, speaking the truth in love, we will in all things grow up into Him who is the Head, that is, Christ. From Him the whole body, joined and held together by every supporting ligament, grows and builds itself up in love, as each part does its work (Ephesians 4:15-16).

The apostle Paul stated in his letter to the Ephesian church that the church is built on the structure of the prophets, teachers, apostles and evangelists (Ephesians 4:11-13). Structure is important; without it, the church cannot hope to achieve its stated goals and purposes. This situation is also true for group life.

Importance for the Group
As important as it is to have a specifically stated purpose or goal for a group, it is useless if it is not linked with an appropriate structure to accomplish the group tasks which are vital to fulfilling its purposes. Thus, it is not surprising to note that having appropriate structures is important for fulfilling group tasks. Appropriate

SMALL GROUP DYNAMICS GRID

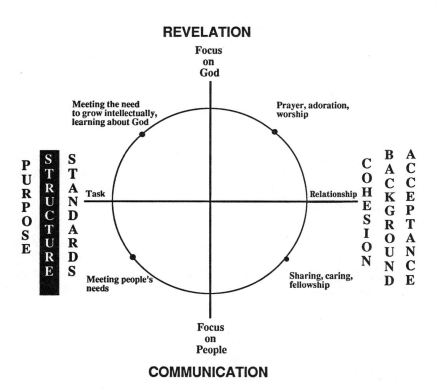

structures are like stepping stones across a river. Without them, you would have a difficult time crossing the river to your destination. You can get there, but it sure is nice to have a path which doesn't lead to getting in over your head.

A structure ought to be appropriate for the task of the group. For instance, it is not nearly as important to define a structure to facilitate small group involvement that keys on fellowship, if the task of the group is to provide opportunities for evangelism. We can determine an elaborate structure to link people with one another, to encourage fellowship between individuals. But if the stated purpose for a particular group is to provide opportunities for evangelism, then the structure doesn't match the purpose. This is obviously true when it comes to constructing buildings. No one builds a kitchen to facilitate sleep. Nor do we build structures into our small groups to provide worship if that is not one of the stated goals for the ministry of that group.

In one small group, the leaders and core members decided to have a stated time in each group meeting devoted to taking five minutes for one person to describe how he or she came to faith in Christ. This structure greatly encourages group members to develop a sense of cohesion and involvement with one another. It is exciting to see such a structure facilitate the sharing and caring within a particular small group.

It is extremely important for the overall life of the group to have such structures built in which facilitate achieving the purposes for the group. Simple structures such as starting and ending times are extremely important for the overall life of the group. It is no use for a group leader to become upset if people are not attentive one-half hour after the stated ending time for a particular group.

Marks of a Healthy Group
One mark of a healthy group is a structure that facilitates its overall purposes. The following examples illustrate this point. Providing time for an individual to share something about his or her life contributes to the overall purpose of linking group members together. Such a structure promotes the idea that sharing and caring are vital to accomplishing the overall goal of establishing a true fellowship of believers.

Another structure that can be built into a group is as simple as a schedule. For example, one night the emphasis is on fellowship and caring; another night the focus is on worship; the next week group members may concentrate on Scripture study; and evangelism is the focus of the fourth week. This kind of structure assures that the group is proceeding toward its stated goals if they include fellowship and caring, worship, instruction, and evangelism.

In one small group, the stated structure included a potluck supper whenever there was a fifth Tuesday in a month. This schedule provided a festive spirit among the group members at least four times a year. Such a regular structure allowed the group to anticipate these evenings as a part of the regular group life. Instead of holding potluck suppers at random, although that is a viable option, they were built into the regular structure. The group recognized that gathering for a common meal nurtures the well-being of the group and its individuals, as well as contributing to the stated goal of providing for sharing and caring.

Another way of defining a structure is simply to plan the meetings. When such a plan is communicated to the group, it is understood as being the overall guide for the evening. Although some people believe that if meetings are too structured we hinder the work of the Holy Spirit, this does not have to be the case. If a plan for an evening is viewed as an overall guide and not a rigid device that takes control of the group, this structure aids the group and does not control it. Groups that do not have such a plan flounder and do not accomplish the tasks that need to be done. A formal plan or structure yields benefits for the group if it is clear and understood.

In addition to a formal structure, another mark of a healthy group is the ability to incorporate the informal structure without impeding it. For example, a group may have an informal structure that encourages members to gather in the kitchen for fellowship once the meeting is finished. The formal structure may indicate that the group's formal meeting is over; but then the informal structure takes over, pointing to refreshments in the kitchen. Everyone knows that it is generally the plan to pack the kitchen to the maximum for food and interaction. At this point, the formal structure indicates when it's time for the informal to take over, but it doesn't impede it.

Guidelines for Leaders

First, the leader needs to determine the formal structure that will guide the overall group. In order to do so, there are several questions that need to be asked and answered:

- With reference to a formal structure, will there be a stated starting and ending time? And if there is such a structure, is it communicated to group members?
- Is there a sequence for the evening that will help facilitate meeting the stated goals and purposes of the group? If there is a stated sequence, is it really going to achieve what we have set out to accomplish?
- How will we handle the times when the formal structure seems out of place with the particular spontaneous events of the evening?
- Will we follow a plan for a stated length of time, e.g., the next three months? If so, how will we determine it? What can we do to make that plan a reality?

Once a formal structure is determined, it is important to communicate it to the group members. If the group understands why things are done the way they are, then it will be easier to follow the stated structure. After it is communicated to the members, then the next step is to enforce that structure.

One of the most frustrating aspects of a group's formal structure is the starting time for meetings. It is all too common in some groups for people to walk in after the stated starting time. There are several ways of dealing with this situation. It is clear that the formal structure must be enforced, but the question is how. One group leader decided to provide very little acknowledgment of the member who arrived late and to comment to him about the importance of coming on time. The result was resentment and frustration for the group member and frustration for the leader. The small group member was resentful because of the perceived insensitivity of that leader. The leader was frustrated at the apparent lack of concern on the part of the member for the need of the group to get started on time.

A formal beginning time is very easy to enforce if the group begins the meeting at the stated starting time no matter who is there (assuming the leader came on time!). When people do come in afterwards, they are welcomed and made to feel at home within the group. But the leader does not necessarily have to review everything that has gone before. It is not fair to those who have come on time to start ten minutes late in order to give the latecomers a chance to arrive. To do so is a slap in the face to those who have made quite an effort to get there on time, perhaps even skipping dinner. Starting on time does not mean that we consider latecomers second-class citizens since we do not know the reasons why people come late.

Another abuse of the formal structure is the domineering member. For example, Mary was frustrated at the apparent disregard for the group that a certain member exhibited. Mary was thorough in her preparation and had diligently provided for times of sharing personal needs and concerns. But inevitably John was the first to jump in and say, "These are my concerns." And for the next 5 to 10 minutes he dominated the entire group, telling his needs and prayer requests in deep detail to the detriment of others who wished to share. There was no time after John talked for other people to share their own needs and requests.

The formal structure was in place. Mary had done her job in providing time for adequate sharing and prayer requests, but John abused the structure. The appropriate way of handling this issue is not to abandon time for prayer requests but to enforce a stricter, specific structure on how they are shared. If it is clear that people are to identify their prayer requests in a short sentence or two, then such a specific structure can be enforced. Times can be included in groups to encourage deeper sharing, but such abuse of guidelines must be checked.

The last guideline for the leader is to observe the informal structures which exist in these small groups. If the small group seems to have a desire for hanging around after the formal meeting to chat with and pray for one another, this action should be recognized and maximized. Time on the formal level can be cut back to allow for the informal times of sharing and caring and interaction. The group leader needs to focus on the overall ministry, taking into account what happens outside of the formal structures of that group.

Another example of such an informal structure is the way people spontaneously reach out to one another to meet needs. If there is a need for providing meals for a sick member of the group, it is certainly appropriate to have a formal structure to meet it. But some groups just naturally provide for such needs without any formal prompting. In an informal way, they have a structure for handling those needs. The leader should be alert for such structures and maximize them when they aid the group's purposes.

Review and Reflection
1. What formal structures exist in the group(s) to which you belong?
2. What structures should be built into your group?
3. What time restraints do you have to follow? Are these recognized and adhered to?
4. Is the structure of your group too predictable, not predictable enough, or just right?
5. Do people in your group know what structures exist? What informal structures do you recognize?
6. Is there a structure that militates against the stated goals of the group? If so, how can it be changed?
7. In what areas must you enforce an already existing, agreed upon structure in the group? How will you do so?

SEVEN

THE RICHNESS OF PEOPLE'S BACKGROUNDS

There is neither Jew nor Greek, slave nor free, male nor female, for you are all one in Christ Jesus (Galatians 3:28).

Even though it happened a long time ago, the lesson God taught Peter is very contemporary.

About noon the following day as they were on their journey and approaching the city, Peter went up on the roof to pray. He became hungry and wanted something to eat, and while the meal was being prepared, he fell into a trance. He saw heaven open and something like a large sheet being let down to earth by its four corners. It contained all kinds of four-footed animals, as well as reptiles of the earth and birds of the air. Then a voice told him, "Get up, Peter. Kill and eat."

"Surely not, Lord!" Peter replied. "I have never eaten anything impure or unclean."

The voice spoke to him a second time, "Do not call anything impure that God has made clean."

This happened three times, and immediately the sheet was taken back to heaven.

While Peter was wondering about the meaning of the vision, the men sent by Cornelius found out where Simon's house was and stopped at the gate. They called out asking if Simon who was known as Peter was staying there. . . .

Peter went down and said to the men, "I'm the one you're looking for. Why have you come?"

The men replied, "We have come from Cornelius the centurion. He is a righteous and God-fearing man, who is respected by all the Jewish people. A holy angel told him to have you come to his house so that he could hear what you have to say." Then Peter invited the men into the house to be his guests (Acts 10:9-23).

In Peter's day, Gentiles did not associate with Jewish people, nor Jewish people with Gentiles. Their backgrounds prohibited interaction between the two groups. Yet in a profound vision to Peter, God made His point: If God has cleansed someone, it is not our business to call him or her unclean. And indeed it would be wrong to do so. Peter apparently got the hint for he went with the Gentiles to interact with Cornelius. Cornelius, of course, responded to the message of the Gospel and believed in the Lord. Peter stated, "I now realize how true it is that God does not show favoritism but accepts men from every nation who fear him and do what is right" (Acts 10:34). Peter learned the lesson, but have we?

Importance for the Group

Our small groups must be havens for people from all kinds of backgrounds, not just for people who are like us. Recognizing the importance of others' backgrounds affects the cohesion of the group. Group members will not be linked together unless there is an appreciation of everyone's background. This fact means that socioeconomic status or culture should not affect whether or not we accept a particular person. Different cultures may cause difficulties, but at no time are we to reject a person because he is not part of our culture.

One of the most vibrant groups that I have ever seen consisted of

SMALL GROUP DYNAMICS GRID

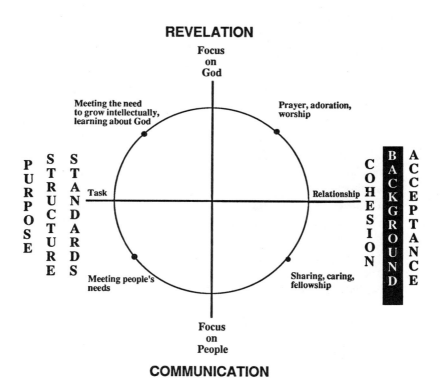

people in their 20s, 30s, 40s, 50s, and 60s. Some people came from educated backgrounds that carried high status, such as physicians. They fellowshipped right along with those who were retired and making very little money.

What group members focused on and encouraged was a recognition that they are all one in Christ and no one is better than another simply because of worldly standards. The leaders, Dick and Cindy, were able to guide the group into one of the liveliest and most nurturing groups I have ever seen. Affirming, rather than denying, their backgrounds benefited and unified the group.

However, the flipside of this issue is the tendency to form cliques and subgroups within a small group. A clique does not help to establish good group life. Cliques exclude. A subgroup, on the other hand, is a normal grouping of individuals who do not carry the air of exclusivity.

Cliques are to be avoided at all costs. The small group is not a place for several cliques to form and discuss their relative worth in light of the other cliques that exist in the group. The small group exists to foster the unity that Jesus desires for us. This goal may involve some subgroups. That is, people with similar interests and backgrounds may get together to discuss some common concerns. But the focus is always on the overall health of the group. Whether or not the subgroup is able to exchange information and ideas is secondary. Subgroups are important to the group; cliques are devastating.

Different backgrounds not only affect the group's cohesion but also its perspective. For example, Pam led a group in a part of the city where a wide range of community issues, such as hunger, poverty, and homelessness, dominated the scene. Pam's background was such that she really desired to help these people. Her past experiences contributed to an empathy for individuals who were less fortunate than she was. It was amazing that many people in her group also shared a similar concern and had experience working with individuals who needed help in a very practical way. The result was that the perspective of the entire group was colored by their concern for those less fortunate.

This was not a bad situation. In fact, it was quite good as Pam was able to rally support, concern, and involvement of the whole group to address some of those community issues. In this case, the group's perspective was colored by each person's background. That is, many of them had experience in dealing with people less fortunate than they; and the group was naturally inclined to help such people. It is not surprising, then, to see that this perspective actually adds a richness to the group's resources.

Thus, if we view backgrounds as sources of richness and resources, we can appreciate them as a positive element in a small group rather than a divisive one. This is not to say that there aren't occasions when a person's background causes real problems and concerns. Certainly this is true. However, if we can turn the situation around to appreciate individuals' backgrounds for the sake of the group, then we are able to use them for the group's benefit.

Recently I was discussing the issue of starting on time with a colleague who worked with our Laotian ministry. It was fascinating to view the way background affected tolerance, planning, and goals. For my colleague, who was thoroughly Western in orientation, starting on time was very important. When he met with his Laotian brothers and sisters, their view of time was different from his. This situation could have led to frustration in working with this group. However, it really highlights the issue that background affects our standards. What one background may consider rude, another may consider as normal. Thus, starting on time was not terribly important to the Laotian ministry. They were more interested in focusing on relationships. If a person shows up half an hour late (late as far as Western standards reckon it), it is not nearly as important as recognizing that the person showed up at all. So we can see that a person's background does affect the kind of standards he or she will place upon a group of individuals.

Marks of a Healthy Group

A healthy group recognizes the importance of diverse backgrounds. The group also recognizes the richness of those backgrounds. Thus, in some groups, people discuss their backgrounds, how they affect the resources they bring to the group, and how they influence their view of the group's standards and procedures.

Having discussions about people's backgrounds enables us to use those resources when there are group needs. So when we discuss guidelines for leadership, we should be able to recognize the function of those backgrounds and promote or prompt members to discuss them. Every background has elements which are both good and bad. We should accentuate the positive and not dwell on the negative.

To do so involves the critical element of acceptance. People who come from other religious backgrounds may feel insecure in an existing small group. Thus, it is important not to criticize a person's background, but also to offer a listening ear to understand it and realize that there probably is some richness in it. To accept another's background does not mean we necessarily have to endorse everything he says or brings from it. Acceptance says, "I accept you as a person regardless of what kind of background you have."

It is obvious that a person's background can add a tremendous amount of richness to a small group. This fact reminds me of Jim, who has a tremendous ability not only for organizing but also for getting tasks done. Jim is the perfect person for a small group to call upon when there is a project that needs to be tackled. Because of Jim's professional background and personality, he is able to work diligently on projects and complete them. A group leader has only to assign the task, and Jim can be counted on to get it done—and on time.

Recognizing backgrounds is particularly important for those in task groups. Task groups by definition seek to accomplish a particular goal, are usually short-term, and have a specific completion date for a particular task. Debbie joined a task group; and after only two meetings, the group was calling on resources from her background. The resource she brought to the group was employment in the food service industry. As a result, she was able to acquire food at a very reasonable cost for a social event for couples. Debbie was also able to provide a vital link to accomplish the task for the group.

In listening to other people's backgrounds, then, we must be very careful to communicate both acceptance and understanding. As people share where they have come from, others in the group can be alert for possible resources. And because people's backgrounds affect the standards and procedures they consider normal, it is important that the group discusses and clarifies the procedures that are necessary for a particular small group.

Guidelines for Leaders

A group leader can take time to discern people's backgrounds. A simple question like, "What do you appreciate about your upbringing?" can prompt group members to discuss and appreciate other people's backgrounds. The same type of question can be asked about people's religious backgrounds. There is much to learn from other people's experiences of Christianity as children. This does not mean we always need to affirm what was learned, but we can recognize the value of the positive parts of these backgrounds.

When a group is to participate in a project, a leader can inquire about any special talents or training that could aid the group. Just recently I was discussing group leadership issues with Mark. He was beginning as a new leader of an existing group, a group he had been part of for several years. I expressed my desire to have several groups get together and rehab a house in one of the low-income areas of the city. I hadn't realized that Mark had worked on such a project last year. He had experienced what it takes to get it off the ground. Because of his own area of expertise in the trades, he had contact with many others who had a strong desire to serve in this very practical way. Had I not found out his background, I never would have been able to ask Mark to pursue this project. But it took time for me to get together with him to discuss his life and vision.

This experience highlights what is perhaps the most important aspect of maximizing people's backgrounds. Leaders must be willing to invest time to find out about their group members' backgrounds in order to be able to call upon their built-in resources. Although it takes time, effort, skill to draw out this information, and insight to match need with skill, every leader can do this with his group members. Everyone brings some knowledge or skill from his background that he can contribute. But sometimes leaders need to dig to find a need to match to the resource, or to find the resource to match a need.

Review and Reflection

1. What in your own background is helpful for the life of your group?

2. What backgrounds of individuals in your group can you identify? Do any bring resources that can be utilized now?
3. What can be done within your group to identify backgrounds and accompanying resources and strengths?
4. In what ways are the group members' backgrounds less than helpful to the group?
5. Should you adjust the structure of the group to give more time for discovering backgrounds? If so, how can you restructure the group?

EIGHT

COHESION: GLUE TO BOND PEOPLE TOGETHER

As a prisoner for the Lord, then, I urge you to live a life worthy of the calling you have received. Be completely humble and gentle; be patient, bearing with one another in love. Make every effort to keep the unity of the Spirit through the bond of peace. There is one body and one Spirit—just as you were called to one hope when you were called—one Lord, one faith, one baptism; one God and Father of all, who is over all and through all and in all. But to each one of us grace has been given as Christ apportioned it (Ephesians 4:1-7).

It is no secret that Scripture teaches us to live in community and not just as individual believers. Paul's emphasis in Ephesians 4 is for believers to recognize how they are bound to one another—bound by some common elements and by their participation in the Holy Spirit. For as believers, we all have the Holy Spirit living in us. We have a bond in our baptism and follow one Lord. We exercise the same faith and call upon one God and Father of all. And we

SMALL GROUP DYNAMICS GRID

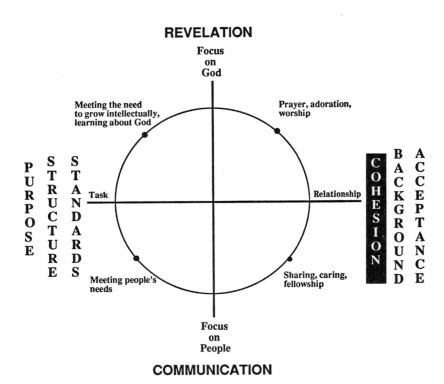

each have received grace from Jesus Christ.

Importance for the Group

These things knit believers together. As it was then, so it is also to be now for our small groups. Developing a sense of unity or cohesiveness is vital. The overall purpose of our lives is to glorify God and live in community with other believers. When we look at the overall tasks or purposes for our small groups, we realize we can't do them alone. We must have the unifying factor of the entire group participating in achieving those purposes.

This unity will not come from people's backgrounds, although similar ones can certainly lead to it. But unity will come from a common faith, a common bond in Christ, and a common recognition of the need for one another. If we recognize our commonality, then we are able to cooperate with one another in fulfilling the tasks for which a group is gathered.

Even the overall Christian witness of a group is affected by how we demonstrate unity or cohesiveness to the outside world. If the world constantly observes strife and bickering within a church or small group, then the witness is tarnished. We ought to be individuals who are not afraid to live with one another, care for one another, and achieve our purposes alongside one another. The world marvels when such cohesiveness exists among diverse people.

Such cohesiveness is also essential for our individual well-being. As we recognize how we are interrelated, we also experience a sense of well-being in knowing that others deeply care about us. It is another way of saying that people are showing their acceptance for us because they have bound themselves to us. The unity that we have does not mean we disappear as individuals into a sea of other people. Rather, we maintain our individuality and have it affirmed by other believers. It is not an individuality that is arrogant and sits on the sidelines; but it is a well-being, a deep feeling of worth because we belong to one another and others have committed themselves to us. We, too, have that common bond with other people.

Within a small group, it is vital that the members see unity and cohesiveness as extremely important for the well-being, not only of the group, but also for themselves. Any attempt to break up the group's unity should be resisted. The human body is an excellent example for us. It is a wonderful model of how unity is achieved in the midst of having diverse members. Yet anything that might threaten that unity, such as disease, kicks in an immune system which seeks to ferret out the intruder.

Marks of a Healthy Group

And so it must be for a healthy group. Anything that seems to threaten the overall unity of the small group must be resisted. However, there is also a recognition that cohesion does not mean that group members must all be similar. Indeed, the church is not that way. The beauty of the body of Christ is that we are all different and yet have a fundamental unity. This unity is maintained not because we are different but simply tolerate one another. Rather, it is obtained because we share a common bond in Christ, share the Spirit, and have a common faith. Thus, any group that works on this cohesiveness will draw upon the strength that comes from a common confession, a common faith.

Occasionally, however, disruptions do happen. Yet the group needs to discern whether or not a particular disruption or person is actually threatening the unity of the group or simply moving it on to a new sense of vulnerability and care. Such is the difference between what I call destructive criticism, which seeks to tear down and divide, and healthy, constructive criticism which seeks to move the group on to higher heights.

Nonetheless, these disruptions do, in fact, occur often in groups. As a body reacts to disease, discerning whether what is occurring is growth or invasion, so also the group leader — or a group of people with responsibility for a small group ministry — must discern whether what is occurring here is growth or invasion, that threatens the very unity and cohesiveness of the group.

Consequently, the leader must recognize the cohesive factors of the group. For instance, people's backgrounds, such as similar education, can be a binding force for a group. For example, I encouraged two physicians to attend a particular function of the small group ministry of which I am in charge. It was not surprising to observe that these two doctors had found each other and began to discuss medical situations. Both of their backgrounds provided a link to each other and a certain cohesion at that point. There is,

98

however, a danger that such cohesion can lead to a clique, a situation of which the leader needs to be aware.

Another binding factor for a small group is the leader. If there is a sense of unity with reference to the leader, a recognition that what the leader does is helping the group, then the group is bound together more effectively than if there is a constant bucking of the leader's direction.

A third cohesive factor is the overall task of the small group. A common task, common goal, common target provides a tremendous sense of unity for the group members as they work together.

Guidelines for Leaders

A group leader can teach and guide the group to understand the biblical teaching on unity. A discussion of the different types of spiritual gifts in 1 Corinthians 12 may be threatening for some. But the basic point of the chapter is recognizing how God has wonderfully designed the church to provide a maximum of diversity, through the gifting of the Holy Spirit, while maintaining a maximum of unity in Christ.

As a part of recognizing the unity we have in Christ, leaders can also teach what the church affirms in the area of doctrine. Common convictions breed community. People who adopt a set of teachings as their own are affirming that they belong to one another by virtue of their confession. Rather than being boring, lifeless material, doctrine can be exciting and should be made interesting as the group studies it.

Group leaders can also urge their members to help each other in a crisis. In so doing, the group will be unified in accomplishing a set goal. Remember the discussion of Bill who developed cancer? His entire small group rallied around him and Susie, providing people to cook meals, scrub floors, do laundry, and run errands. The sense of cohesiveness was greatly enhanced through such a crisis. We don't go looking for crises, of course; but we know that God can bring good things to a group through one.

Group contracts also aid cohesion. If a group agrees on certain times, procedures, structures, etc., and binds their agreement in a written covenant, they are immediately bound to one another in ways not usually found in the world. A group contract need only state the basic understanding of why the group exists and how members will participate. This doesn't, of course, have the tone of a legal agreement. It is only expressing on paper the desire that people have to gather in community for the benefit of each other. See the sample covenant on page 101.

Even shared experiences provide glue for the group. Thus, if group members work together on a major project, a sense of cohesiveness develops. Even as people go through crises, the group can rally around them in order to let them know the group is behind them. What we are talking about is simple investment in one another's lives, whether it is in a leader or in a member who is going through struggles. The result is a unified front against anything that might cause the group to fray. The leader, therefore, must determine how these cohesive factors can be maximized and what kinds of situations will enhance such unity.

COHESION: GLUE TO BOND PEOPLE TOGETHER

BEGINNER GROUP COVENANT*

For the next six weeks, we agree to the following disciplines as a group:

Attendance: To give priority to the group meetings.

Participation: To give yourself to the purpose of the group—to get acquainted and become a spiritual community—by sharing your "stories" with one another.

Confidentiality: To keep anything that is shared strictly confidential.

Accountability: To give permission to group members to hold you accountable for goals you set for yourself.

Accessibility: To give each other the right to call upon one another for spiritual help in times of temptation and need—even in the middle of the night.

Evangelization: To keep the door to your group open to others in your church who need help.

SPECIFICS:
We will meet on _____ (day of week).
We will meet at _____ (place).
The meeting will begin at _____ and close at _____ .

GROUND RULES: What do we want to do about . . .
    Refreshments _____
    Baby-sitting _____
    Newcomers _____
    Absence _____

I will try with God's help to be a regular, faithful, caring member of this group.

HOW DYNAMIC IS *YOUR* SMALL GROUP?

Signed: _____

NAMES OF GROUP MEMBERS: PHONE:

_____   _____

_____   _____

_____   _____

_____   _____

_____   _____

_____   _____

_____   _____

*From *Search the Scriptures* by Lyman Coleman (1983: Serendipity House).

Review and Reflection

1. In reviewing the needs and concerns of your group(s) what has helped to develop group unity or cohesion?
2. What Scripture texts further illustrate the need for cohesion?
3. Can you name a time when the group seemed particularly unified? When was it, and why did it have a large sense of cohesion?
4. Are there people in your group who either add to unity or, possibly, detract from it? How can you encourage the ones who enhance unity and minimize the effect of those who militate against it?
5. What can you add to your group to promote a greater sense of unity?

NINE

STANDARDS FOR PROCEEDING
AND EVALUATING

*Let us examine our ways and test them, and let us return
to the LORD (Lamentations 3:40).*

Nehemiah was deeply moved by the plight of his countrymen, the
Jews, who were back in Jerusalem. He himself was in exile as a
servant of the king. But King Artaxerxes granted him the opportunity to go back to Jerusalem to help rebuild the city walls. In his
book, Nehemiah told the story of how he arrived in Jerusalem and
began to survey the situation:

*I went to Jerusalem, and after staying there three days I set
out during the night with a few men. I had not told anyone
what my God had put in my heart to do for Jerusalem.
There were no mounts with me except the one I was riding
on.*

*By night I went out through the Valley Gate toward Jackal
Well and the Dung Gate, examining the walls of Jerusalem,
which had been broken down, and its gates, which had been*

destroyed by fire. Then I moved on toward the Fountain Gate and the King's Pool, but there was not enough room for my mount to get through; so I went up the valley by night, examining the wall. Finally, I turned back and reentered through the Valley Gate. The officials did not know where I had gone or what I was doing, because as yet I had said nothing to the Jews or the priests or nobles or officials or any others who would be doing the work.

Then I said to them, "You see the trouble we are in: Jerusalem lies in ruins, and its gates have been burned with fire. Come, let us rebuild the wall of Jerusalem, and we will no longer be in disgrace." I also told them about the gracious hand of my God upon me and what the king had said to me (Nehemiah 2:11-18a).

The story of Nehemiah is vitally important for group leaders. Those who are planning for small group ministry can learn much about leadership from this man of God.

Importance for the Group

Nehemiah understood the necessity of examination and the importance of applying standards and procedures to his life. When he set out to examine the wall of Jerusalem, he knew what it should look like. He evaluated how it did look and found it wanting. He understood that his goal was to build up the wall and that God would graciously help him do it. Nehemiah had standards that he applied and procedures that he followed in rebuilding the wall.

Standards and procedures are a wall of protection in small group ministries. Such standards are important to the group in that they provide a necessary avenue for accomplishing the appropriate tasks.

Bill, a small group leader for many years, knew that part of his responsibility was to encourage people to share their lives with one another and to develop a prayerful mindset in dealing with one another's needs. As a result, two of the standards he set for the group were providing time for sharing prayer requests as well as guidelines for such sharing. It was not uncommon in Bill's group for people to break off into groups of three or four and go into other rooms of the house in order to share what God had been doing in

SMALL GROUP DYNAMICS GRID

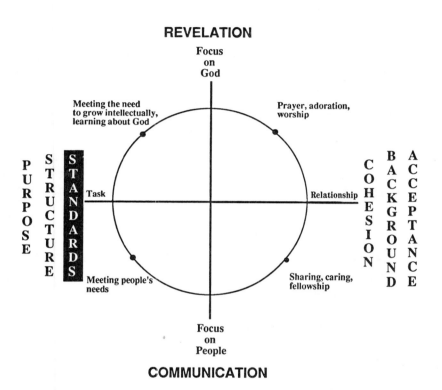

their lives, specifically and individually. They were able to ask, "What are the concerns that we have which we can join together in praying about?"

Bill's guidelines also included admonitions like, "Make sure that your prayer requests are to the point and that you are giving other people a chance to share their needs." Bill also urged them to make sure they did indeed pray at a group meeting and not just simply talk about their prayer requests. Bill knew the importance of procedures and standards when trying to fulfill the task of getting members involved with and praying for one another.

Effective standards and procedures also provide a safe climate in which people can operate. If, as in the case of Bill's group, people know that they will have an opportunity to share a concern or a need because it is part of the group's procedure, then there is less chance that they will interrupt at an inappropriate time in the meeting. Procedures provide a level of safety for those who wish to share. They know they will be given time and attention.

This safety is true with other tasks as well. If part of a group's task is worship, then a procedure needs to be established to provide the appropriate avenue for such worship. Procedures do not restrict this activity; instead, they provide people with a safe atmosphere in which they can engage in adoration and praise of God.

Agreed-upon standards and procedures also lead to greater cohesion within the group. A great deal of cohesion leads to safety as well. Since the group's standards and procedures have been discussed and agreed upon, the group has a certain bonding, even if it is only the bonding of sharing these common instructions. Certainly the cohesion goes beyond that once people begin to achieve the tasks and build the relationships that are so vital within a small group. Before those relationships are formed, the group knows, at least initially, how to operate because they share the common element of those standards and procedures.

It is not surprising, then, that having appropriate procedures helps a group follow through in group communication. This, in turn, enhances the positive forms of communication and squelches negative, destructive forms.

Marks of a Healthy Group

First, a group agrees on standards and procedures. Members do not necessarily have to discuss every standard and adopt it by vote, but each group needs to affirm that they indeed will follow the standards and procedures. Whether the group as a whole has formed them or not is not nearly as crucial as having the group adopt the procedures.

Secondly, group members must understand all the ramifications of those standards and procedures. For instance, if members of a group such as Bill's wish to pray at any time during the meeting, they haven't understood the reasons for the guidelines Bill established for an appropriate prayer time. Once such reasons are understood, people are more likely to follow these standards.

This is true, for instance, when a group is beginning to study the Scriptures together. If some members are constantly going off on tangents, then others can become very frustrated. However, the leader can draw people back by saying, "Listen folks, I know that one of the things we want to do as part of our regular group meeting is to get through at least most of the questions that relate to the study of the evening. I know it would be nice to be able to address all the questions you have, but we don't have time. Perhaps we can deal with some of these issues at another time, but right now let's concentrate on the task at hand in order to get through the designated questions."

Most people are glad to curb some of their comments that are at best tangential. There is a sense of well-being that comes through the completion of the tasks at hand. Those within the group who hinder the accomplishing of those tasks are generally not appreciated either by the leader or by the other participants. The problem may be that the set standards and procedures have not been understood.

Discussing and understanding the group's standards is not enough, however. They are worthless unless the leader and others urge the group to follow them. The group leader or another person can be a watchdog, so to speak, for the entire group in order to keep them moving toward the appropriate goals. A watchdog urges the group not to become sidetracked through lack of attention to the stated procedures. This situation is not synonymous with rigidity; it only means that common concerns decided upon ahead of time are followed.

Standards may need to be modified, however. Thus the group ought to be open to doing so. For example, a group may adopt the procedure of rotating the responsibility for the Bible study. This method may be appropriate for a period of time, but it may need to be modified at some future date. Doing so need not be threatening; it just means that it is time for a change.

Such change need not be resisted. Changes in structure, standards, and procedures can be exactly what a group needs to provide a good healthy sense of excitement. Stuart Briscoe, Senior Pastor of Elmbrook Church, in discussing worship, declared, "Predictability breeds boredom, but unpredictability breeds anxiety." We must keep a healthy balance between those sets of structures, standards, and procedures which lead to a sense of well-being and yet be careful that they don't lead to boredom.

Guidelines for Leaders

First of all, a leader must decide who will set the standards and procedures the group will follow. She may let the group determine them or do so herself, perhaps consulting several people for feedback. Involving others contributes to the accomplishing of tasks and building relationships that are so necessary for a small group.

Once standards and procedures are determined, the leader must communicate them to the group. This may be done in several ways. One is to hand out a set of guidelines which the group will follow. Another possibility is to take 5 or 10 minutes at the beginning of each meeting to review some of the standards and procedures and to introduce new ones if necessary.

After communicating them, it is also important to discuss the implications of those standards and procedures and how they should be enforced. Having a procedure that is not enforced is worse than not having one at all. Enforcement, of course, should be gentle but firm. If an action does not conform to a procedure, it should be pointed out in an appropriate manner and resisted at the appropriate times. Finally, the leader must change procedures when necessary. Usually this action is done with the involvement and interaction of at least a few key people from the group.

There are other facets a group leader should consider in developing standards and procedures. The following questions help to focus the issues more sharply:

- How will we make decisions?
- How will we know when to speak?
- Can we interrupt each other?
- What will the role of the leader be? Should he be strict about keeping us on track? Is it all right to go off on tangents?
- How open can we be with each other? Is this meeting confidential? Will we discuss our needs with those not in our group?
- Is it all right to miss a meeting?
- How long should we meet? Six weeks? Six months? One year?
- Must we always study the Bible? Pray? Discuss?
- Must we always have the same format?
- Is our group open to newcomers?
- Are there guidelines we should follow when sharing prayer requests?

Answering these questions, along with others you may think of, will help a group establish appropriate standards and procedures. Since they are vital to a group's effectiveness, any time spent on them is worthwhile.

Review and Reflection
1. What are the stated standards and procedures that your group follows?
2. Are there standards and procedures that must be added to make your group more effective? What are they, and how will you implement them?
3. Are there any standards that have, in your opinion, hurt the group? What are they, and how will you adjust them?
4. Are there repeated violations of these standards and procedures with which you need to deal? How will you or the leader do this?
5. In your evaluation of your group(s), what standards and procedures are helping you to meet your goals? What is counterproductive?
6. What other standards and procedures, which are not mentioned in this chapter, would help your group?

TEN

THE SMALL GROUP LIFE CYCLE

Not that I have already obtained all this, or have already been made perfect, but I press on to take hold of that for which Christ Jesus took hold of me. Brothers, I do not consider myself yet to have taken hold of it. But one thing I do: Forgetting what is behind and straining toward what is ahead, I press on toward the goal to win the prize for which God has called me heavenward in Christ Jesus (Philippians 3:12-14).

The small group is a dynamic organism going through stages of life much like the stages of human life. In the case of human beings, we are not surprised that people pass through different levels of understanding and ability. Two-year-olds are not expected to have the same tolerance level as 32-year-olds. In small group ministries, we should likewise not expect a recently formed group to "have its act together" in the same way as a long-standing group. This chapter examines these stages to promote understanding of, and patience with, small group ministries.

Birth

The first step for any small group is its forming. With any new venture, there is a profound lack of ability in many areas that are considered crucial for group life. In time these develop, just as children grow. We must give them lots of attention and care at this point. The group members may meet basic requirements, but they aren't too sure what to expect beyond that.

At this stage, group members recognize the basic purposes of the group and agree to pursue them. The group begins to show signs of life in the sharing and caring aspect and tries to accomplish the tasks for which it was formed. There is acknowledgment of leadership and authority. Yet the leader must give extra care at this point to give firm but gentle direction. Those overseeing the leaders must also give directions to handle such a fledgling group. A new leader may need very specific directions, almost to the point of telling them what to say. Constant contact should be maintained with the leaders at this time.

Early Childhood

After the fragile state of having just been formed, the group moves into the exciting time of early childhood. There is rapid growth in pursuing the goals for which they are gathered. Relationships are kindled; there is growing excitement about the people in the group. Group members wish to please the one in authority, whether leader or pastor.

Some childhood characteristics occur during this period. First of all, there is always the possibility of some sibling rivalry between brothers and sisters in Christ. People don't know each other well enough to develop real personality conflicts, but there is sufficient annoyance at this stage to provoke some uneasiness. Another childhood characteristic that can creep into the group is a short attention span or short commitment. We should not be surprised if some try the group for a short period of time and then disappear. This is normal.

Nonetheless, even with the prospect of these characteristics, there is growing excitement about developing relationships within the group. The group is an exciting place to be, just as the world is exciting for a young child.

Adolescence

The adolescence period is unpredictable. A small group may go through some growing pains. There may be a questioning of values or purposes which were held dear earlier. There may even be some questioning of authority of those overseeing the group, although it may not manifest itself openly. There may be just a bit of resistance when leaders give directions.

There also may be some form of passivity. While group members may have been deeply involved in the ministry of the group prior to this, some will now choose to let the leader do everything. They tend to sit on the sidelines to watch. They attend but add little to the meetings.

The group often struggles with the awareness of the needs of individuals and the group itself. Individuals may demand the attention of the group, saying, in essence, "Look at my needs *now*." Yet the group has a task. Group members could become divided at this stage wondering how to minister to those with great needs while maintaining the focus of the group as a whole.

One group at this stage is led by Bob and Jean who also started the group. In the beginning, there was great excitement as people met to form this group. Bob and Jean desired to build Christian values and understanding into the lives of several young families. The momentum of starting was enough to carry them for months.

The leadership style appropriate for this stage is coaching. Some direction may be necessary, but overall suggestions, which are then carried out by the group or leader, may be all that is necessary. The group begins to take on some responsibility for itself. In fact, members will try anything. But the maturity and skill levels are not quite to the point of releasing the group to independence from close oversight.

After Bob and Jean's group went through the exciting stage of beginning to develop relationships and grow in the faith, a certain disgruntlement appeared. Bob and Jean became uneasy. Several members preferred to conduct their own business in the group without the knowledge of the leaders. Things were planned behind Bob and Jean's backs. In essence, there actions were a denial of the authority structure of the group. In the end, Bob and Jean became frustrated with the group's stage and stepped down from being leaders. Yet this was just a phase. The group is now rapidly developing into the next phase: adulthood.

Adulthood

We could identify several stages of adulthood. There is the early adulthood stage of a group when it thrives on the challenges of group life. There is a growing awareness of one another's abilities and faults. Lasting friendships are developed. The group begins to take full responsibility for its actions and pursues the purposes of the group with a passion.

Bill's group is experiencing the joy of this stage right now. Group members sense a great love for God and for each other. They desire to please God at all costs. Just mentioning a need in the group results in it being met. The group is unified in what it is trying to do. In fact, other leaders look in envy at Bill's group, wishing theirs were like it. The truth of the matter is that most groups go through this phase. We need only to patiently nurture them to it.

Groups in the early and middle stages of adulthood have depth of character and commitment. In a word, they are mature. This does not mean there are no newcomers, but the group knows how to handle them well. Leadership development also is apparent at this stage. A good leader begins to give many opportunities for others to lead various parts of the meeting. People are really beginning to identify and use their spiritual gifts.

Later Adulthood

With the onset of later adulthood, a group may find offspring leaving the nest. Leaders who have been developed in the group find new opportunities for ministry in other groups. It may be that some who started the original group are now functioning in a daughter group elsewhere. Plus, the group has a sense of wisdom.

Nevertheless, the group's passion may wane a bit. There may be less fervor to accomplish the tasks necessary. The group, in its familiarity with one another, may forget about basic group tasks. In so doing, members may become a bit less patient with one another.

Group leadership at this point may be characterized by the word *delegation*. People are fully capable of handling nearly any area of group life. The leader has done his job of enabling others to lead.

Death

Although we try to deny it, some groups die. Though painful, it is normal. There are two options at that point. We can attempt a resurrection or bury the group. Resurrection is possible, but rare. One group, led by Mike and Martha, went through one. Just when they had experienced the apparent loss of a group which had been meeting for a long time, a new wave of life brought in a fresh vision. New people came to regenerate the group, and the dead parts either fell away or were revived.

This kind of change did not happen to Debbie's group. It also had been going for a long time. But Debbie became increasingly frustrated by the lack of response in the group. People had become comfortable. They were not interested in aggressively pursuing the goals of the ministry. Attendance was sporadic; in fact, at times, no one came. In the end, it was obvious that the group should not continue.

Although Debbie still carried some guilt, thinking she was the cause of the death, the truth was that she had no part in it. Debbie was encouraged to let go since she could not have lengthened the life of the group. In fact, the group was dead even before she recognized it. God had performed mightily through Debbie during the group's life. Now it was time to bury the group and remember what God had done through them.

I have found that burial is the most common result of such groups. Resurrections don't occur that often. It is better to start new groups and urge those who have been a part of a dead group to start again in a new situation. In so doing, they leave behind the deadness and begin to breathe in the freshness of new life.

Guidelines for Leaders

A few guidelines may help leaders at this point. They can save themselves a lot of worry by recognizing that group stages are temporary. A new group will not show the depth of the adult group, but give it time. Leaders can take heart in the natural process of group living. Certainly we wish to train group members to grow and mature. But then we must let them go and do it!

In the course of group life, there may be a need to correct behavior with a firm hand. This is especially true early on. Young groups need a lot of direction from a leader. It is better to lead somewhere and be criticized for it than to wait for group members to exhibit all the qualities which make them particularly useful. Surely, a group in early childhood can't cope with the same responsibilities as those in adulthood. But the group can accomplish something.

Group leaders should also recognize that growth is seldom achieved at a constant rate. The differences of rates at different stages of the group is frustrating. Nevertheless, we must remember that we are merely workers; God causes the growth.

Review and Reflection
1. What stage is your group at right now? How should this affect your leadership?
2. What other characteristics, which qualify as part of a particular stage, can you identify?
3. What factors lead to the demise and death of a group? Do you agree that death of a group is natural? Why or why not?
4. How can a group leader minimize the negative effects of early childhood? Of adolescence?

ELEVEN

PUTTING IT ALL TOGETHER

Consequently, you are no longer foreigners and aliens, but fellow citizens with God's people and members of God's household, built on the foundation of the apostles and prophets, with Christ Jesus Himself as the chief cornerstone. In Him the whole building is joined together and rises to become a holy temple in the Lord. And in Him you too are being built together to become a dwelling in which God lives by His Spirit (Ephesians 2:19-22).

Now that you understand the elements of small group dynamics, do you have a vision of how they link together to maximize the effectiveness of groups for God's kingdom? Groups that practice these principles can look forward to great fruitfulness. So in order to put them into focus, this last chapter contains several situations which can be improved through applying these small group dynamics.

Small Group Case Studies

For each of the following cases, ask yourself: Which part of group anatomy is affected? What is unhealthy in the situation? What can the leader do to correct the situation? What does the group need to do to correct the situation?

Case #1: John and Sally are upset with their group leader because he repeatedly is critical of people from their former church. They enjoyed their religious upbringing.

It is not difficult to observe the leader's profound lack of appreciation for someone's background. The leader is way out of line in his comments. Unfortunately, he may not be aware of hurt feelings in the group. As a result, John and Sally ought to confront the leader, admitting that his comments have hurt them. The leader deserves a chance to reconcile this relationship — and a chance to clean up his act! Hopefully, the group itself will approach the leader in this regard. If they don't, however, John and Sally must confront the leader.

Case #2: Debbie has been frustrated in the Bible study portions of her group's meetings. Hardly a week goes by without some vigorous disagreement over the interpretation of the Bible.

This case is a bit trickier than the last one since it involves several issues. First of all, apparently there are not sufficient guidelines for the Bible discussion time. Questions for group discussion may lead to such disagreements, but a healthy group will major on what is most important in a biblical text and not on extraneous issues. Specific, well-focused questions dealing with the text at hand may help avoid these disagreements.

Secondly, the group may not be aware of the backgrounds of individuals who disagree. A "plain meaning" of a text may not be so plain to those with different upbringings. In addition, the leader may need to take some control at this point. He can model acceptance with the added comment that the group could discuss this issue for a long time, but they need to get back on track to finish the study.

The group may also need to give attention to the responsibility of accepting one another and communicating to edify one another. A standard of communication may need to be established. Disagreements can occur. But on relatively minor issues, let us not disagree in such a way that we forget to honor one another with our speech.

Case #3: Paula, the Bible study leader, is considering resigning from her role as teacher because fewer than one-half come prepared for any given meeting.

The question that immediately comes to mind in this case is, "Is this a stated expectation or only an implied expectation?" If it is only implied, then Paula should either make such an expectation explicit or check her frustration at the door. If the expectation is explicit but people are not complying, then it is appropriate to ask whether or not it is reasonable. It may be that the standard is set far too high. If the group determines that the standard is reasonable, then group members should discuss their own responsibilities with the group leader.

Case #4: John and Joan are looking for a different group because (1) they have observed that Bill and Jan, the current group's leaders, are not speaking to Mark and Cheryl; and (2) no one else in the group seems to be concerned.

This case is difficult. The difficulty is not in identifying the area of group dynamics that is affected but rather in determining how to handle the situation. John and Joan need to be encouraged to share their concern with the leaders, Bill and Jan. This action will clarify whether or not it is only their perception of the situation or if the leaders recognize it too. If Bill and Jan admit their difficulties, it is their responsibility to make it right with Mark and Cheryl. Their lack of acceptance of these two is affecting the group negatively, even if group members do not admit it. If John and Joan get no response from the leaders, then it is time to contact those in charge of the leaders, possibly a pastor or deacon, if such a structure exists.

Value of Small Group Involvement

Recognizing the value of group dynamics will pay off in the overall ministry of the groups. In closing this chapter and, subsequently the book, I urge you to consider the effectiveness of small group ministry in the Christian community. Elmbrook Church took a survey of 3,000 adults to examine congregational attitudes and practices. People who were involved in small group ministries were more likely to be using their gifts and were more meaningfully involved in the church. They studied their Bibles more often, witnessed of their faith in Christ more often, and had developed relationships at a far greater rate than those without any group involvement. In short, group involvement provides needed enrichment to the church of Jesus Christ. So let's do everything in our power to maximize its effectiveness.

Review and Reflection
Solve the following case studies:
1. Cynthia privately complained to her group's leaders because she was irritated that Trudy talked so much in the meeting.
2. Mike wants to have a time when the group can give Phil, the group leader, some feedback about his leadership style. Mike thinks Phil has too much control over the group and wishes to control the meeting by opening it with the question about Phil's methods.
3. Steve and Ingrid have been unhappy because the Bible study time has been postponed the last three weeks. Each time someone had a "crisis" he shared with the group for nearly 45 minutes, taking up the time allotted for both sharing and Bible study.